# WEST MAUI

## A NATURAL HISTORY GUIDE

ANGELA KAY KEPLER

Mutual Publishing

Library of Congress Cataloging-in-Publication Data

Kepler, Angela Kay, 1943-
  West Maui : a natural history guide / Angela Kepler.
    p. cm.
  Includes index.
  ISBN 1-56647-823-5 (softcover : alk. paper)
  1. Natural history--Hawaii--Maui--Guidebooks.  2. Maui (Hawaii)--Guidebooks.  I. Title.
QH198.H3K478 2007
508.969'21--dc22
                                        2006038608




ISBN-10: 1-56647-823-5
ISBN-13: 978-1-56647-823-6

First Printing, July 2007
1 2 3 4 5 6 7 8 9




Mutual Publishing, LLC
1215 Center Street, Suite 210
Honolulu, Hawai'i 96816
Ph: 808-732-1709 / Fax: 808-734-4094
email: info@mutualpublishing.com
www.mutualpublishing.com


Printed in Taiwan

---

**Previous Page: Peeking above layers of silvery clouds, West Maui's glorious ridge tops are captured here through a telephoto lens from high on Haleakalā. ' Īao Valley lies to the left; Waihe'e to the right.** Cameron Kepler

# TABLE OF CONTENTS

# ACKNOWLEDGMENTS

Over the years numerous people contribute to the evolution of a book. To all who have expressed aloha to me—biologists, outdoor enthusiasts, the Hawaiian community, friends, and acquaintances from all walks of life—I extend my warm appreciation. Special thanks are due to the US Fish & Wildlife Service, Sierra Club, Mauna ʻAla Hiking Club, Mary Evanson, Bob Hobdy, Derral Herbst, Art Medeiros, Stephen Mountainspring, and Bob Gustafson for hiking opportunities and companionship under rugged

A superb brown stingray (*Dasyatis latus*) cruises gracefully among a school of blue-lined snappers (*Lutjanus kasmira*) at the Maui Ocean Center in Māʻalaea.

conditions. I offer grateful thanks to Tom Hauptman (Pacific Helicopters) for superb and courageous flying skills.

Lucienne de Naie (Sierra Club, Maui Tomorrow) exuberantly kept me up-to-date with new conservation happenings in West Maui, as did various employees of Hawaiʻi State Natural Reserve System, The Nature Conservancy, Randy Bartlett, and Hank Oppenheimer. Chris Brosius (West Maui Mountains Watershed Partnership), Dale Bonar and Scott Fisher (Maui Coastal Land Trust), Ed and Puanani Lindsey (Project Mālama Honokōwai/Maui Cultural Lands, Inc.), and Maui Nui Botanical Garden (Director Lisa Schattenburg-Raymond) opened their doors widely in true Hawaiian fashion.

It is always a pleasure to feature other photographers; I hope that their pleasure matches mine. Special thanks to Bob Abraham, Randy Bartlett, Pat Bily, Bishop Museum Archives, Blue Hawaiian Helicopters, Dale Bonar/Maui Coastal Land Trust, David Boynton, Tim Burr, Ron Chapple/Blue Hawaiʻi Helicopters/MCLT, David Davis, Betsy Gagné, Haleakalā National Park, Harrington Photo/Kapalua Bay Hotel, Hawaiʻi Department of Natural Resources, Hawaiʻi State Archives, Bob Hobdy, Alan Holt/The Nature Conservancy, James Hudnall, Jim Jacobi/USGS, Darren Jew/Maui Ocean Center, Kāʻanapali Beach Hotel, Cameron Kepler, Kīlauea National Wildlife Refuge, Ron Nagata, Nakamoto Art Studio, Jack Noble/Greenpeace, Hank Oppenheimer, Pacific Whale Foundation, Douglas Peebles, Pierre of Lahaina Studios/Lahaina Restoration Foundation, Ed Robinson, Frank Rust, John Severson, Brett Simison, Rob Shallenberger, Walter Steffan, Tim Sutterfield, Wailea Destination Association, and Robert Western.

And finally, my deep gratitude extends to my aloha-filled husband, Frank Rust, for his constant encouragement, patience, and assistance with digital photography.

# PREFACE

From royal blue ocean depths, through sandy and rocky shorelines, over iridescent foothills, deeply precipitous mountain valleys, rising to mist-gathering elfin forests, the diverse representation of West Maui's ecological life zones exemplify the quintessential ahupua'a of ancient Hawai'i. This traditional Polynesian concept embraced a long triangular slice of sea, shore, coastal lowlands, lower foothills, and inner valleys to the highest mountain tops. This was Hawai'i's sacred 'āina. As in a jig-saw puzzle, every component was necessary for human living, every component was vital for constant forest regeneration, for life-giving fresh waters, for healthy and bounteous reefs and adjacent seas.

*West Maui: A Natural History Guide* describes the entire mass of West Maui, beginning in Wailuku and extending in a full counterclockwise circle past Mā'alaea and the Pali tunnel, along the coasts and hills south of Lahaina, and the prestigious tourist resorts of Kā'anapali and Kapalua. From here, the narrow, muddy, tortuous road is barely drivable but the chapters continue, although ideally driven from the Wailuku side.

The precipitous headwalls of 'Īao Valley: a hiker's view from a knife-edged ridge close to Pu'u Kukui (5,788 feet). Chief Kahekili's son deserves a medal for scaling such cliffs barefooted (see Chapter 2). Bob Hobdy

This publication does not recommend restaurants, hotels, shows, or rental car agencies. It was written with the sincere hope of introducing readers to little known aspects of West Maui. You will see native plants in gardens and public parks. Observant eyes will find endangered coastal herbs, rare traditional Hawaiian bananas, delicate native jellyfish, marine turtles, whales, and reef fish. On special occasions, the ancient crafts of spear throwing, complex lei making, nose flute playing, outrigger canoe racing, and tapa beating can be found.

Cameron Kepler

An elegant West Maui specialty plant, the 'Eke silversword (*Argyroxiphium calignis*) shines in silvery glory amid a montane bog above 5,000 feet elevation.

It is my hope that this book will engender a gentle awareness of West Maui's magical energies: where light energy manifests as a rainbow arching over an inland valley, where wave energy curls in turquoise translucence within sheltered bays, where wind energy daily shapes cloud patterns gathering over land and sea. Behind these idylls, many devout, personal energies are alive in West Maui, maintaining healthy reefs and clear inshore waters for fishing and snorkeling, and also for the reef denizens themselves, so they may continue to live and multiply. West Maui's small but stunning montane forests, now more than ever, need public sensitivity and hands-on management to survive.

A beautiful, rare traditional Hawaiian banana, Mai'a (Maoli) Manini (*Musa acuminata X balbisiana AAB*), photographed at Maui Nui Botanical Garden. Also called Mai'a Koa'e, A'ea'e, or Hawaiian Variegated banana.

Most potent of all energies is the impalpable energy of love in its innumerable forms. Individual love revitalizes us as we relax amidst beautiful surroundings...yet in a broader perspective, an even richer, embracing love can partner with knowledge to enlighten us to greater depths. The aim of this book is to engender or enhance this latter type of love for West Maui's

'āina, especially for those who may be new to Maui and do not understand the fragility of our island ecosystems and cultural ways. My fervent hope is that these pages will act as mālama, an enlightening, guiding light for those who live in, work in, and visit West Maui's stunning circular landmass.

Today, West Maui is poised on the threshold of unprecedented changes. Let us all love her wisely, making sage decisions for her future, constantly aware that both her sparse, fragile natural resources and remnant traditional Polynesian culture need vigilant nurturing.

Transported to Hawai'i as "canoe plants," mountain apples still thrive deep in moist gullies of West Maui. In addition to eating, fruits and bark were used medicinally.

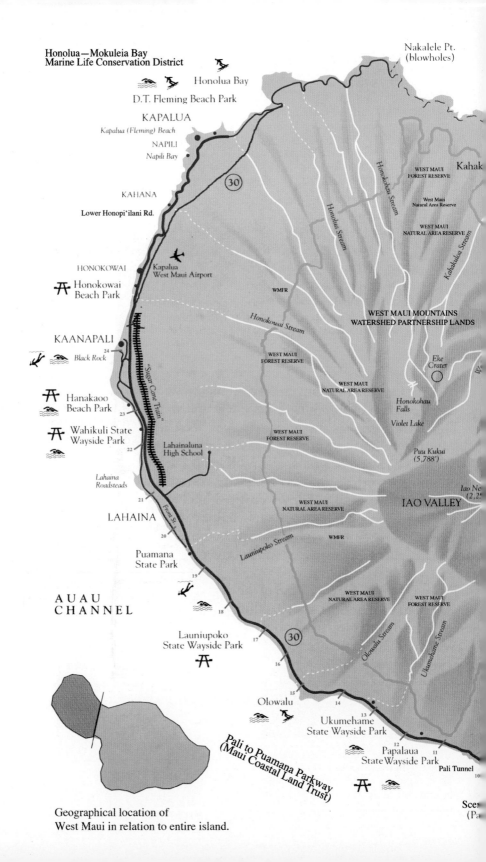

Honolua—Mokuleia Bay
Marine Life Conservation District

Honolua Bay

D.T. Fleming Beach Park

KAPALUA

*Kapalua (Fleming) Beach*

NAPILI

*Napili Bay*

KAHANA

Lower Honopi'ilani Rd.

HONOKOWAI

Kapalua
West Maui Airport

Honokowai
Beach Park

KAANAPALI

*Black Rock*                24

Hanakaoo
Beach Park                  23

Wahikuli State
Wayside Park                22

*Lahaina
Roadsteads*

                            21

LAHAINA                     20

Puamana
State Park                  19

A U A U
C H A N N E L               18

Launiupoko
State Wayside Park          17

                            16

                            15

Olowalu                     14

                            13

Ukumehame
State Wayside Park          12

Pali to Puamana Parkway
(Maui Coastal Land Trust)

Papalaua
State Wayside Park          11

Pali Tunnel                 10

Nakalele Pt.
(blowholes)

Kahak

WEST MAUI
FOREST RESERVE

West Maui
Natural Area Reserve

WEST MAUI
NATURAL AREA RESERVE

*Honolua Stream*

*Honolua Stream*

WMFR

*Honokohau Stream*

*Honokowai Stream*

WEST MAUI MOUNTAINS
WATERSHED PARTNERSHIP LANDS

WEST MAUI
FOREST RESERVE

WEST MAUI
NATURAL AREA RESERVE

*Eke
Crater*

*Honokohau
Falls*

*Violet Lake*

WEST MAUI
FOREST RESERVE

*Puu Kukui
(5,788')*

"Sugar Cane Train"

Lahainaluna
High School

Front St.

*Launiupoko Stream*

WEST MAUI
NATURAL AREA RESERVE

WMFR

WEST MAUI
NATURAL AREA RESERVE

WEST MAUI
FOREST RESERVE

IAO VALLEY

*Iao Ne
(2,2*

*Olowalu Stream*

*Ukumehame Stream*

*Kahakuloa Stream*

30

30

Sce
(Pa

Geographical location of
West Maui in relation to entire island.

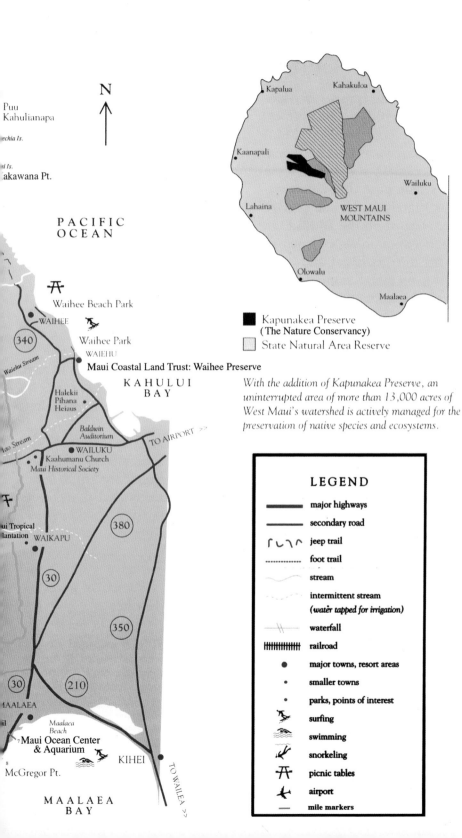

Puu
Kahulianapa

echia Is.

i Is.

akawana Pt.

N

↑

PACIFIC
OCEAN

⛩
Waihee Beach Park

WAIHEE 🏄

Waihee Park
WAIEHU

340

Waiehu Stream

Halekii
Pihana
Heiaus

Baldwin
Auditorium

Iao Stream

● WAILUKU
Kaahumanu Church
Maui Historical Society

KAHULUI
BAY

TO AIRPORT >>

ᚦ

ui Tropical
lantation

WAIKAPU

380

30

350

30        210

IAALAEA

il ●

Maalaea
Beach

7 Maui Ocean Center
& Aquarium

McGregor Pt.

🏄

KIHEI ●

TO WAILEA >>

MAALAEA
BAY

Kapalua ●        Kahakuloa

Kaanapali ●

Wailuku ●

Lahaina ●        WEST MAUI
MOUNTAINS

Olowalu ●

Maalaea ●

⬛ Kapunakea Preserve
(The Nature Conservancy)
▨ State Natural Area Reserve

Maui Coastal Land Trust: Waihee Preserve

*With the addition of Kapunakea Preserve, an
uninterrupted area of more than 13,000 acres of
West Maui's watershed is actively managed for the
preservation of native species and ecosystems.*

## LEGEND

| | |
|---|---|
| ▬▬ | major highways |
| ── | secondary road |
| ⌐⌐ʌ⌐ | jeep trail |
| ············ | foot trail |
| ～ | stream |
| ⌇ | intermittent stream (*water tapped for irrigation*) |
| ╫ | waterfall |
| ‖‖‖‖‖‖ | railroad |
| ● | major towns, resort areas |
| • | smaller towns |
| · | parks, points of interest |
| 🏄 | surfing |
| 〰 | swimming |
| 🤿 | snorkeling |
| ⛩ | picnic tables |
| ✈ | airport |
| — | mile markers |

# CHAPTER 1 WAILUKU

Wailuku (pron. wy-loo-koo), although an active business center and county seat (Maui County also includes Moloka'i, Lāna'i, and Kaho'olawe), still retains some of the sedate pace that characterized pre-statehood Hawai'i (before 1959). Nestled on the alluvial fan spilling out from 'Īao Valley, it merges eastward into its larger and more modern twin town, Kahului (right). Life in its back streets is unhurried, and many residents still carry on family traditions of working with the land, a legacy of the old sugar plantation days.

Listen and watch carefully for living Asian customs. You may see a group of elderly ladies taking a break from gardening, chatting in their native tongue, or an old man strolling home from the market carrying his daily bundles of taro leaves, imported Japanese seaweed, and daikon (a long white root vegetable like our cucumber).

Wailuku, gateway to the famous 'Īao Valley (pron. ee-yow), is a charming mix of old and new. There are historic sites, ethnic restaurants (Thai, Chinese, Korean, Japanese), food to-go, cultural activities, lovely shade trees and a health food store. Here well-dressed lawyers mingle with Buddhist priests, "hippies," demure Japanese secretaries, and Filipino mechanics.

Wailuku (population 12,000) possesses a variety of architectural styles ranging from the nine-story county building—so distinct you can spot it from the air—to tumbledown, tin-roofed shacks. Expansive mountain views offer a change from the ubiquitous Hawaiian beaches.

Wailuku's Farmer's Market is also popular with those who enjoy fresh garden produce often grown organically. Watch for unconventional fruits such as jackfruit and lychees.

**(opposite) Part of Wailuku's Historic District, Ka'ahumanu Church was named after the powerful chiefess and wife of King Kamehameha I, Queen Ka'ahumanu (1768–1832). An ardent promoter of Christianity, she owned the first New Testament printed in the Hawaiian language. After attending services in 1832 in a grass shack on the present church site at the corner of High and Main streets, she asked that a permanent church be built and named after her. Unfortunately, the resulting adobe structure was poorly cemented and eventually dissolved in the rain. Today's charming New England-style edifice, with its steeple clock, dates from 1857. Its pews are made of koa, a prized native wood.**

Many venerable trees still beautify this "top end" area of Wailuku such as monkeypod (*Samanea saman*).

The old Iao Theater holds many memories of fine performances for Maui's kama'āina community.

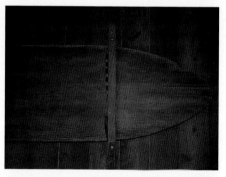

Duke Kahanamoku's original (1916) surfboard is one of the treasured displays at the Maui Historical Society Museum. Perhaps the most well-known Waikīkī surfer-cum-beachboy of all time, Duke was indeed a truly international athlete, having won a gold medal in the 100 m freestyle Olympic Games swimming event at Waikīkī in 1912.

Many Wailuku residents still grow taro and vegetables in their backyards.

The Maui Historical Society Museum: Hale Hōʻikeʻike or House of Display (pron. ha-lay hoe-eekay-eekay) is the renovated home of Edward Bailey (1814–1903), an early missionary, artist, poet, sugar miller, and teacher. Set amid spacious grounds and mature shade trees, this museum imparts a sense of tranquility. It transports us to bygone days by way of missionary items such as nineteenth century furniture and handmade quilts, and artifacts from stone-age Hawaiʻi, including tapa cloth, koa calabashes, and poi pounders. Special exhibits are presented periodically. Listed in the National Register of Historic Places, it was built in several stages between 1833 and 1850. Its 20-inch-thick stone walls did not suffer the same fate as the original Kaʻahumanu church, as Mr. Bailey knew the secret of adding goat hair to the mortar to act as a binding agent. The museum is located on the left side of Main Street (Route 32) as you drive up to ʻĪao Valley.

This old canoe, built in traditional Hawaiian style from a single koa log, sits in an open shed beside the museum. The orange paint is not traditional; however the original hull would have been lacquered with paʻele, a black mélange of banana bud sap, kukui (candlenut) inner root bark, and burned pandanus or wiliwili (Hawaiian coral tree) roots. Such a mix temporarily preserved the wood against sun and salt.

# Maui Nui Botanical Garden

Maui Nui Botanical Garden, created in 1976, specializes in native and Polynesian introduced plants (200 species and varieties). Since many of Hawai'i's native, endangered plants originated in coastal areas, it provides ideal habitats for sand- and salt-tolerant species. Of the canoe plants, it specializes in sugarcane (kō), bananas (mai'a), taro (kalo) and sweet potatoes ('uala). The garden, located on Kanaloa Avenue in Kahului, bordering Wailuku, is also one of Maui's community cultural, horticultural, educational, and environmental centers.

Hawaiian cotton or ma'o (*Gossypium tomentosum*), endemic to Hawai'i, produces sparse, brown, fluffy fibers. Although a lowly plant favoring arid, rocky coasts, crossbreeding research with commercial cotton saved the latter from massive losses due to insect damage.

Hawaiian poppy or pua kala (*Argemone glauca*) is related to the opium poppy. Early Hawaiians recognized its anesthetic properties by mixing its pounded seeds and sap as a toothache cure.

Bird's-nest fern or 'ēkaha (*Asplenium nidus*) is an elegant, symmetrical fern reaching six or more feet in diameter.

A selection of Hawaiian cordage made at the Garden.

(left) Hawai'i's traditional Manini, Koa'e, A'ea'e or Hawaiian Variegated banana is one of the most stunning banana varieties in the world. (right) The only green-and-white variegated Polynesian variety in existence, its jazzy, striped fruits are here carefully lowered by the Garden's Director, Lisa Schattenburg-Raymond.

(left) A truly Hawaiian and Polynesian delight is the sight and taste of these traditional Mai'a (Maoli) Manini (native) bananas. Note their full, rounded tips and long, sausage-like shape. They are delicious when sautéed in butter and garlic, especially if also drenched in coconut cream. (right) The Garden's 40-variety sugarcane (kō) collection includes this stripy curiosity, well named Hapai, or pregnant.

(left) The famous paper mulberry tree or wauke (*Broussonetia papyrifera*), originally from SE Asia, and transported to Hawai'i during spurts of eastward and northward colonization, grows well at the Garden. (right) Nine-year-old Emily Alexander concentrates while carefully beating bark cloth (tapa or kapa) made from the inner bark of wauke.

(left) Of Hawaiian ancestry, Lietta Kuanoni skillfully twists the strong, silky inner bark of the wild hibiscus or hau tree (*Hibiscus tiliaceus*), a coastal plant growing naturally all over the Pacific. These same strands comprise the famous Tahitian and Cook Island dancing skirts. (right) A Polynesian nose flute musician, Anthony Natividad crafts his own flutes in different sizes and tonalities. The flute's haunting sounds are remarkably clear.

(left) Fourth generation kamaʻāina, or old-timer, and lei maker, Maile Yepis descended from a well-known early missionary family, the Baldwins. Here she displays a just completed lei using native leaf shoots ʻūlei (*Osteomeles anthyllidifolia*) and hinahina (*Artemisia australis*) to complement the spidery flowers of dwarf poinciana (*Caesalpinia pulcherrima*). (right) Ti or ki leaves (*Cordyline fruticosa*) and red ginger bracts (*Alpinia purpurata*) interweave along a braided, "rose-ey" ti-leaf strand.

Hawaiian endemic Kokiʻo ʻula (*Hibiscus clayi*).

Hawaiʻi's state flower, the saffron-hued maʻo hau hele (*Hibiscus brac-kenridgei*), near-extinct in the wild. Like all members of the hibiscus family, it grows easily from cuttings. It is also frequently offered at the Garden's plant sales and giveaways.

Andrew Binkley learns Hawaiian spear throwing from Jay Laʻa. In olden times, banana trunks were indeed substituted for human sacrifices!

**Maui Nui Botanical Garden's labeled sugarcane (kō) collection (40 varieties) is a statewide treasure. (left to right) Honomalino, Halāliʻi, Moano, Mahaiʻula, ʻAkoki, ʻUala lehu, Uahi a Pele kanalima, Uahi a Pele, Lahi, Manulele, Pōhina, Waiʻōhiʻa, ʻIeʻie, Kō Kea, Honuaʻula, HC63, Waimea, Uhu, Kalaloa, Pokapua, Laukona, Nānahu, Laukona, Lauloa, ʻUala 61, ʻIeʻie, HC62, ʻĀwela, Laukona, and ʻIeʻie.** Lisa Raymond and Tina Barnes / MNBG

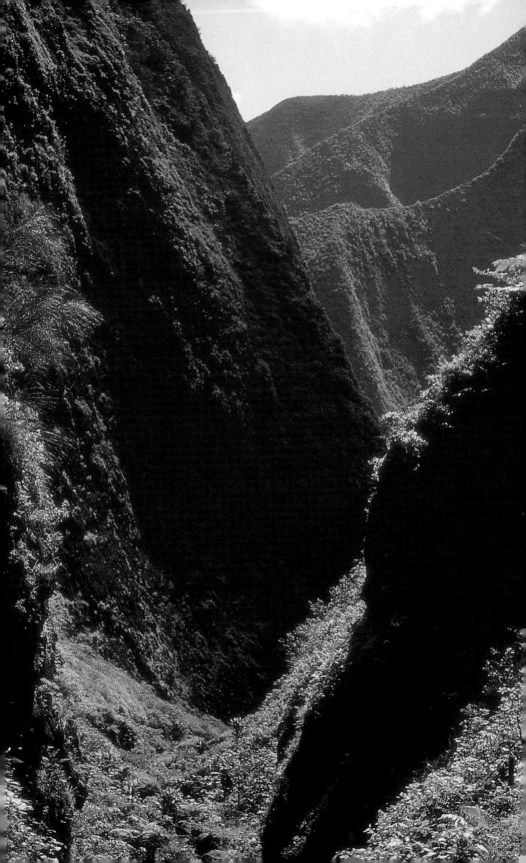

# CHAPTER 2 'ĪAO VALLEY

West Maui's magnificent mountains—a ring of precipitous, knife-edged ridges and deep, narrow valleys—are accessible only by Route 32. Eighty years ago, the verdant journey from Wailuku to 'Īao Valley took three hours; today a car makes the trip in about five minutes. 'Īao Valley State Monument, a six-acre park and botanical garden with views into the heart of the massif, is spectacular. Park your car, cross the bridge and walk up the steps to the 'Īao Needle Lookout, then stroll along the shady riverside trail. On clear days, the valley's headwalls and West Maui's highest peak, Pu'u Kukui (5,788 feet, pron. poo-oo koo-koo-ee), rise in glorious splendor, marking the location of an extinct volcanic crater. This entire valley is not only stunning but it is sacred to the Hawaiian people—please respect it.

Frank Rust

**Kūkaemoku or 'Īao Needle (cloud supreme), spiring to 2,250 feet, dwarfs two walkers on the bridge spanning 'Īao Stream.**

**(opposite) A hiker's view from inside the dark valley east of 'Īao Needle, visible on the right from the staircase lookout. These picturesque valleys have been carved out of volcanic rock entirely by streams.**

# Kepaniwai Park & Heritage Gardens

This delightful streamside picnic area en route to the ʻĪao Valley State Monument is maintained by the county as a tribute to Maui's multiracial society. Ethnic pavilions are dedicated to Filipinos (bamboo house), Hawaiians (thatched home, somewhat dilapidated), American missionaries (New England-style house), Koreans (decorated archway right), Portuguese (villa with arbor), and the Chinese and Japanese (landscaped dwellings). Picnic tables and barbecue pits are covered in case of rain (at least 75 inches of rain falls here annually).

The name Kepaniwai (pron. kay-pan-ee-wy) commemorates the bloody defeat of Maui's chief, Kahekili—a pivotal event in Hawaiʻi's history. In 1790, Kamehameha I, having begun to unite all the islands by force turned his gaze to Maui. Landing in Kahului Bay, he drove Kahekili's forces up into the heart of ʻĪao Valley. Maui's brave warriors, decimated by deadly war clubs and spears of shark's teeth, fell by the hundreds, choking the stream and turning it red. The name Kepaniwai

was thus born: damming of the waters. The village downstream became Wailuku, or water of destruction.

Kahekili's son apparently escaped by scaling a 3,000-foot precipice at the back of the valley. This perilous "short cut" to Lahaina, the dream of many hikers, should only be used in a similar emergency.

Monstera or Swiss cheese plant (*Monstera deliciosa*), with huge, multifingered, leathery leaves (up to a yard across) is a tropical import from Mexico's humid rain forests.

The Chinese pavilion with ceremonial lions. Here is a memorial to Dr. Sun Yat Sen, founding father of the Republic of China, who first lived on Maui in Kula as a teenager in the 1880s. Chinese immigrants first arrived in Hawai'i in 1852.

Dwarf pomegranates (*Punica granatum var. nana*) symbolize an abundant life.

Lychees (*Litchi chinensis*), a "giant" in Chinese culture, rarely fruit in Maui.

Hong Kong orchid tree (*Bauhinia x blakeana*), a brilliant rose-magenta hybrid and floral emblem of Hong Kong.

(above and below) Ketembilla or Ceylon gooseberry (*Dovyalis hebecarpa*) is a Chinese favorite. The weeping willow-like bush bears pointed, ruffly edged leaves and purple velvety fruit, pleasingly acidic.

# Filipino Pavilion

Filipino laborers first arrived in Hawai'i in 1906. This cleverly designed, thatched bamboo hut illustrates their many skills. Filipinos, like all Hawai'i's Asian immigrants were—and still are—hard workers.

A clump of bamboo here is a reminder of the importance of bamboo in construction, crafts, food, and everyday life back in the Philippines.

Mabolo, Velvet apple or Philippine fuzzy persimmon trees (*Diospyros discolor*) are rare in Hawai'i. Around October, the ripe orange-brown, fuzzy fruits fall. Their delicious, peculiar flavor is best appreciated when chilled.

An elegant Hawaiian hut—a Polynesian-style meeting house rather than a home—is thatched with fan palms. Slightly raised off the ground, it is adorned with traditional canoe plants: coconut palms (niu), breadfruit ('ulu) , taro (kalo), and ti (ki). Everyday homes were shaped differently, having slanted, pili grass thatched roofs which touched the ground.

Frank Rust

Wetland taro flourishes in special terraces (lo'i), through which running water always trickles.

(above) Breadfruit ('ulu), although less of a staple than taro in old Hawai'i, is nonetheless a dietary item for many Hawaiians, even today. Its taste varies according to its ripeness and variety: the riper, the sweeter and more gooey.

# Japanese Pavilion

Frank Rust

Japanese pagodas and stone lanterns commemorate the 75th anniversary of the first Japanese immigrants to arrive in Hawai'i (1868, 1885).

Howard Brownscombe

A life-sized statue of a hardworking couple, with garden tools, was erected during the centennial year (1985).

(above) Every ethnic site is replete with cultural symbols; the Japanese are no exception. In April, you will see—remarkably!—cherry blossoms from the Okinawan flowering cherry (*Prunus*, Sato-zakura Group), and *matsu*, Japanese black pine (*Pinus thunbergii*). Domestic koi or carp swim lazily in the meandering streamlet.

Newly built for a 2003 centennial of Korean arrival in Hawai'i, this elaborate pavilion is modeled on South Korea's magnificent Bulguksa Temple, a World Heritage Site. The eloquent, very Korean plaque ends with "We are the one."

(left) The Southern magnolia (*Magnolia grandiflora*), from the US South, is widely and lovingly cultivated throughout SE Asia and the north into temperate climates such as Korea. (right) The intricate details of under-eave color and design transport the viewer to a mini world where the peace of Gautama Buddha reigns.

The advance party of Christian missionaries landed (very thankfully!) on Hawai'i's shores on April 4, 1820, sponsored by the American Board of Commissioners for Foreign Missions. Today, this cute little home may appear boring, but its style is exceedingly functional: sturdy, waterproof, and capable of being heated by an inside fire. Perfect. Accompanying such a wooden house was a functional vegetable garden, complete with pumpkins, beans, lettuce, beets, and corn. Many of these imported foods can still be grown today at all elevations.

(left) The Chinese banyan (*Ficus microcarpa*) is easily recognized by smooth, gray bark and small, pointed leaves. Branches may be strangely angular when large. Native to the Malaysian area, the species has thrived in Hawai'i for 100 years, but needs a pollinating wasp (introduced in 1938) for fruit development. (right) What more beautiful flower for missionaries to grow in a strange, "heathen" country than the quintessential rose?

What a dramatic backdrop for a Mediterranean-style house, complete with grape arbor! Precipitous and luxuriant—velvety in places—'Īao's ridges and side valleys daily gather Windward mists.

(above) In Hawai'i, cuttings of grape vines (*Vitis spp, mostly V. vinifera*) were set out as early as 1814 by early Spanish residents. A wave of Portuguese immigrants from the Azores Islands in 1878 nurtured more. (right, top) Valencia oranges were also popular, sweet, and juicy. (right, bottom) A Surinam/Hawaiian cherry tree (*Eugenia uniflora*), heavily laden little red "pumpkins," tart but richly tasty.

# Black Gorge

Black Gorge, famed for its natural rock profile of President John F. Kennedy, is the last major side-canyon before you reach ʻĪao Valley parking lot. Although there is some dispute over the Kennedy likeness, there is no question about the natural beauty of this impressive valley. During one or two hours of steady rock-hopping, the hiker becomes progressively dwarfed by breathtaking escarpments, which close in until they are only seven feet apart. Its vertical headwalls, rising 2,500 feet on both sides, are carpeted with velvety mosses and lacy ferns. Water courses such as this are slippery and subject to rockfalls. They are unsuitable for children or inexperienced hikers.

(left) To top off an exciting trek into West Maui's deep recesses, a hiker takes a short, brisk shower. (right) A close view of a dripping bank of maiden hair ferns (*Adiantum raddianum*). Their stems make intricate hats.

'Īao Needle, pointing its cathedral-like spire skyward for 1,200 feet above the valley floor and 2,250 feet above sea level, is the focus of the park. The needle is actually a rounded knob, the termination of a long ridge curving back into misty obscurity. The name 'Īao means "cloud supreme" or "facing the dawn." Since the valley faces directly east, the latter is especially appropriate. According to Hawaiian legend, 'Īao Needle is the pillared remains of a merman who was punished for seducing 'Īao, daughter of the demigod Maui (best known for snaring the sun up at Haleakalā's summit). At right is a view from the lookout at the top of the steps.

At the Needle lookout, be sure to check the steep verdant slopes and dark valley walls for large (30 inches long) graceful white birds. White-tailed tropic birds or koa'e kea (*Phaethon lepturus*), although fish-eating seabirds, customarily cruise around island valleys. They nest on inaccessible ledges in the cliff faces. The early Hawaiians occasionally stitched their soft, white feathers into cloaks, and their slender tails, used in courtship, have been highly valued for centuries. Even in 1900, a single feather commanded $10!

David Boynton

Close-up of the similar Red-tailed tropic bird at its nest. No wonder island people once valued their satiny plumage! Centuries ago Hawaiian paddlers embarked on special long trips to the Northwest Hawaiian islands, specially to collect tropic bird feathers for their chiefs.

Tropical trees and flowers (some labeled) beautify ʻĪao Valley Park and the nearby tropical gardens of Maui. Due to different flowering times, each week provides a new assortment. What beautiful epitaphs for the generations of aliʻi, or Hawaiian royalty, and warriors buried in this sacred valley!

**Hanging lobster claw (*Heliconia rostrata*) in regal attire. Look for them along ʻĪao Valleys' main walkway as you approach the bridge crossing ʻĪao Stream.**

(left) The sweet aroma of pink plumeria (*Plumeria rubra*) is irresistible. (right) Yellow ginger's (*Hedychium flavescens*) fragrant yellow and gold blossoms, produced annually by the millions, cheer roadsides and gardens throughout the state of Hawai'i. Nip off the tubular end of a flower and suck its nectar.

(left) Resplendent in tricolored glory, the Hanging lobster claw (*Heliconia rostrata*), originally from tropical America, dazzles the eye. True flowers project from the colorful bracts. (right) Curved, dangling triangles of reddish-pink distinguish the graceful heliconia, red collinsiana (*Heliconia collinsiana*).

(left) Abundant throughout the lower valley, the African tulip tree (*Spathodea campanulata*) delights visitors and residents alike, but is actually a threat to native forests. (right) The coolness of ʻĪao Stream tickles Leilani Kepler's toes. At low water levels you may splash and swim safely, but after heavy rains the engorged stream turns wild and dangerous.

(left) Wild hibiscus or hau (*Hibiscus tiliaceus*) blooms all year. In old Hawaiʻi, its flower's fleeting lifespan (one day) symbolized a human life. (right) Common guava fruits (*Psidium guajava*) are for all to enjoy.

(opposite) The loop trail along ʻĪao Stream is a pleasant, easy walk. The pale-foliaged trees with maple-like leaves are kukui (Aleurites moluccana). The early Hawaiians made medicine from its sap and candles from the nuts.

# 'Īao Valley Cultural Garden (Mala)

E mālama i ka wai…"Cherish the water." Since 2000, a new cultural garden, Mala (garden, plantation, cultivated field) has sprouted beside 'Īao Stream, appearing as if by reincarnation. Precontact 'Īao Stream along with its sisters Waikapū, Wailuku, and Waihe'e—Na Wai 'eha or The Four Waters—was one of Hawai'i's most intensely cultivated agricultural regions.

**Overview of 'Īao Valley Cultural Garden (Mala), benefiting from 'Īao Stream, just as in old Hawai'i.**

Flower clusters of the ti plant appear in pink or white. Each blossom resembles a tiny Easter lily.

(left) The shiny, strap-like leaves of ti (kī) pepper the entire lower valley. With multitudinous uses, ti is most famous for producing ʻōkolehao, a strong liquor distilled from its fibrous, sweetish roots. (right) Endemic to Hawaiʻi, this native Kauaʻi white hibiscus, Kokiʻo keʻokeʻo (*Hibiscus waimeae*) is truly one of the Pacific's gems. With eye-catching beauty, it is also fragrant, a rare quality in hibiscus. Worldwide, many sweet-smelling hybrid hibiscus have part-Hawaiian "blood."

Hawai'i's endemic māmaki (no English name, *Pipturus albidus*), highly variable in form, favors streamsides. A nonstinging nettle, its leaves infuse to make a soothing tea. Before, its bark was pounded into a coarse, everyday tapa (bark cloth) and cordage.

Only found in Hawai'i, Koki'o (*Kokia drynarioides*), near extinct in the wild, is a federally endangered species in the hibiscus family.

Another canoe plant, kukui or candlenut tree (*Aleurites moluccana*) pervades 'Īao. Identify it by its pale, maple-like foliage, delicate flower sprays, and walnut-like fruits.

A much beloved fern throughout Hawai'i, laua'e—although widely distributed throughout the Pacific—may not be indigenous to Hawai'i. Culturally, it represents romantic love. This clump greets you as you enter the Garden.

In old Hawai'i, burned, oily candles made from kukui nuts provided home lighting.

Although not a canoe plant, balbisiana is a banana species of interest, since although seeded it is one of the original parents of familiar seedless banana hybrids worldwide. The variety in Hawai'i, Pacol, is of Philippine origin, appearing to have arrived here in the late 1800s.

Balbisiana's beautiful male bud spreads its several, colored, unrolled bracts like a ballerina's tutu. Note the whitish-mauve outer and redder, more glossy inner surfaces. This is not a banana to grow in your garden, since it is quite aggressive and impossible to kill!

Balbisiana's fruits give you a surprise when you bite into them: a mouthful of "gravel"! Many aficionados of Hawaiian culture mistakenly believe this banana to be a canoe plant, Mai'a 'Oa. The best places on Maui to see truly Hawaiian traditional banana varieties are the Maui Nui Botanical Garden (see Chapter 1) and Kahanu Garden, Hāna.

*Musa balbisiana* is the most common banana variety planted in public accessible areas in 'Īao Valley. Photo shows a freshly unfurling bud with purple-red female flowers, whose apple-green ovaries will mature into scantily fleshed fruit. Its white pulp is sweet and tasty.

Of ancient Pacific heritage, black 'awa was the most greatly esteemed of all the muscle-melting, soporific 'awa preparations. In the last few years, a renaissance of interest in 'awa has emerged, even to the extent of having awa bars.

(left) Green 'awa is the commonest 'awa (kava in Fiji and elsewhere in the Pacific). A root preparation was drunk primarily for its intoxicating, sleep-inducing pleasure. (right) Kō 'ula is one of many dark red traditional sugarcane varieties (see Chapter 1). In olden days, sugarcane, one of the few sweet tasting food available to the Hawaiians, was used primarily to ameliorate bitter medicinal flavors. Children also loved to suck on its delectable, fibrous stalks: "old-time candy."

Chinese Dwarf, one of Hawai'i's most popular backyard bananas, sports an enormous bunch of long, sweet, blunt-ended fruit which almost touches the ground. Most plants are only 5 to 6 feet tall.

(left) Hawai'i's endemic 'ama'uma'u fern (*Sadleria cyatheoides*), formerly ranging from coastal cliffs to alpine scrubland, is planted here but can be seen abundantly on Halemau'u Trail, Haleakalā National Park. (right) Hawai'i's best loved hardwood, the rapidly disappearing, endemic koa (*Acacia koa*) bears young fern-like leaves, which mature into crescentic, eucalyptus-like leaves (*phyllodes*), technically expanded leafstalks (petioles).

(left) Nestled within a bed of ti leaves, yellow hala fruitlets lie with small pincushion proteas, symbolizing a new beginning. (right) As utilitarian as the coconut palm, hala (Pandanus or screwpine, *Pandanus tectorius*) has sustained Pacific peoples for hundreds of generations. The pineapple-like ripe fruit is composed of dozens of fruitlets (keys), sweetly fibrous.

Hala leaves are naturally spiny-edged, but when stripped, dried, and woven, no man-made fiber can surpass their beauty and "waterproofed" finish. For millennia, Hawaiians and their Polynesian forebears, have woven long-lasting mats from them.

# 'Īao Valley's Hinterlands

'Īao Valley shelters other extremely rare native plants, such as this purple-flowered lobelia (*Cyanea grimesiana*).

Hawai'i is full of surprises. While clambering around 'Īao's steep sidewalls in 1980, botanist Bob Hobdy rediscovered an "extinct" tree. This native, the Maui hesperomannia (*Hesperomannia arbuscula*), bearing golden, thistle-like flowers, had not been seen since the 1860s.

Viewed from the up-valley side, 'Īao Needle presents a less imposing face—a mere bump on the end of a long ridge.

Hawai'i's volcanic rocks, though appearing sturdy, are crumbly and porous, particularly on steep slopes. However, with extreme care, experienced hikers can enjoy "climbing" thrills. This photo shows the view from the slopes of 'Īao Needle. In the distant v-shaped slot lies the main part of 'Īao Needle.

(opposite) Impassable waterfalls and deep pools dot 'Īao Valley's network of streams. As the mountaintops contain very little flat land, heavy rains quickly cause flash floods and treacherous river conditions.

# CHAPTER 3 WAIKAPŪ

Waikapū (pron. wy-kah-poo) village lies three miles south of Wailuku on Route 30. You pass it en route to Māʻalaea and Lahaina as it nestles at the base of the West Maui foothills. Here, amidst a sea of sugarcane—rapidly being converted into housing developments and golf courses—is located an example of what most people come to Maui to see: exotic tropical fruits and flowers. The plantation (below) boasts 120 acres of viable orchards, crop fields, nursery, and tropical gardens. Its Agricultural Village also features aquaculture ponds, craft demonstrations, and pictorial/historical exhibits.

This is one of the very few spots on Maui where you can actually buy fresh tropical fruits, grown right here on the premises. It is possible to visit the orchard and see, for example, macadamia nuts and rambutans growing on the trees. The flower gardens are extremely well maintained, using minimum chemical pesticides.

Steep-sided Waikapū Valley is difficult to access, since there is no road into the privately owned valley. Occasionally hiking clubs (e.g., Sierra Club) are permitted to hike there.

**Dwarf coconuts line the entrance way to Maui Tropical Plantation. Their large nuts produce tasty coconut water.**

Maui Tropical Plantation

**(opposite) The most engaging of all ornamental bananas, pink fuzzy or self-peeling banana (*Musa velutina*) is featured in Maui Tropical Plantation's tropical gardens.** Frank Rust

# Maui Tropical Plantation

(above) Rambutans (*Nephelium lappaceum*) are one of Hawai'i's most favored tropical fruits these days. This Classic Red variety is typically clothed with flexible scarlet spines which are somewhat leathery. (right) Their firm, yet jelly-like pulp is sweet-acid tasting, obviously related to lychees.

Greengold avocados perform well in Hawai'i's lowlands. Their rich, creamy flesh is enclosed in a knobby, leathery skin. Note also the yellow stem "belt."

Santa Catarina bananas are a dwarf variety of the abundant Apple (Brazilian) variety. It's hard to beat their sweet, lemony taste.

(left and right) Hailing from Australia—but now linked with the Hawaiian Islands—macadamia nuts (*Macadamia integrifolia*) are today considered the world's #1 tasting nut. Botanically, they are classified in the protea family (*Proteaceae*), close kin to pincushions, Pink Minks, King, and other proteas from South Africa and grown extensively in Hawai'i for the cut flower trade.

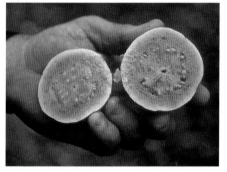

(left) The extraordinarily tough shells of macadamia nuts need first to be baked, then bashed strongly with a hammer. (right) 'Rosy' X 'Supreme' guavas are sizable, pink-fleshed, sweet, slightly acidic, and prolific. They are the same species as the common wild guava, but far superior in taste.

(left and right) Rows of hybrid guava trees (*Psidium guajava* 'Rosy' X 'Supreme') need heavy pruning to time fruiting periods and to control fruit fly infestation.

White Pirie, another meltingly delectable mango—perhaps even better than Haden—is grown on-site at Maui Tropical Plantation. Make sure you have a towel on hand to catch its scrumptiously sweet drips!

To mango aficionados, there is no fruit quite as delicious as a perfect, sun-ripened, deeply golden-fleshed Haden mango (*Mangifera indica*). Originally from India, mangos became so popular in Hawai'i that we now grow over 100 varieties. Unfortunately, mangos sold in most Hawaiian markets are an inferior variety, Tommy Atkins, imported from Central America!

(left) The stunning Jacquinii lobster claw (*Heliconia bihai* ) is prolific and productive. (right) Parrot's beak heliconias (*Heliconia psittacorum*) come in many shades and sizes, making this a polymorphic species. Both heliconias hail from moist, humid rain forests in tropical America.

(left) Bedecked in erotic pink and apple-green, the flamboyant Sexy Pink (*Heliconia chartacea*) secretly sneaked into Maui in the early 1980s as a mislabeled rhizome. (right) Bromeliad gardens at the plantation are simply brilliant. Here the large red-orange *Aechmea blanchetiana* forms a backdrop for *Neoregelia compacta*, a small green-and-pink species which rambles freely.

(left and above) Upright, hot pink banana buds, jam-packed with golden flowers, mature into velvety pink, seedy fruits which actually peel themselves! Fuzzy pink or self-peeling ornamental banana (*Musa velutina*).

(above, left and right) The culinary spice allspice (*Pimenta dioica*) is a beautiful tree, easily identified by its variegated pale bark, fragrant leaves, and clusters of pepper-like berries. Several grow at Maui Tropical Plantation en route to the nursery. (right) A seldom seen aralia (*Polyscias scutellaria*) with round, scalloped, variegated leaves, vies with a huge, deep red hybrid hibiscus (*Hibiscus* hybrid) for attention.

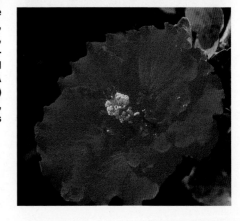

Although the word "ginger" conjures up mental images of the culinary herb, edible ginger is only one of approximately 1,400 species in the family, many of which are extraordinarily attractive. (above left) Red ginger (*Alpinia purpurata*) and pink ginger (above right) are twins of the same species, while the exquisite porcelain shell ginger (*Alpinia zerumbet*) is close kin (below).

# CHAPTER 4 MĀ'ALAEA

Situated in a sheltered sandy cove on the southern edge of Maui's isthmus lies the fishing village of Mā'alaea (pron. ma-ah-lie-ah), only minutes from Waikapū. To reach it, drive Route 30 toward Lahaina and take the cut-off road at mile 6.

Mā'alaea Bay's natural harbor (now altered by a breakwater) has played small but significant roles in Maui's history, During the building of Lahainaluna School in 1831, the first secondary school west of the Rockies, the bay acted as a depository for logs dragged more than 35 miles from Haleakalā's rain-forested slopes. From here, the logs were transported by canoe to Lahaina and upslope to the school.

During World War II, Mā'alaea and the adjacent Gold Coast extending south through Kīhei, Wailea, and Mākena served as strategic training grounds for military activities. All amphibious maneuvers prior to the operations at Iwo Jima and the Marianas were practiced here. In those days, Camp Maui at Kokomo (near Pā'ia) housed 16,000 Marines of the Fourth Division. Their fates were varied: Some married local girls, some earned Purple Heart awards, and some never returned from the battlefields.

Today, Mā'alaea's small boat harbor, once the site of an ancient Hawaiian heiau (religious site) and later a Japanese temple, is jammed-pack with beachside condominiums. Mā'alaea boasts the largest aquarium in Hawai'i, the Maui Ocean Center. Focusing on Hawai'i, visitors to the Maui Ocean Center view exhibits depicting marine life from the surface to the depths of the ocean. The Maui Ocean Center is located in the Harbor Shops at Mā'alaea.

Mā'alaea is one of the few mooring spots on Maui which provides year-round refuge for private vessels, fishing boats, and commercial craft. Charter boats are available here for whale watching, sport and bottom-fishing, snorkeling and scuba diving trips to Molokini, sunset sails, and other cruises. The early morning and late afternoon, when these tours head seaward, are the best times to enjoy the sparkling waters and distant views of Haleakalā that Mā'alaea offers.

Seldom seen in the wild, seahorses can be closely enjoyed at the Maui Ocean Center.

(opposite) A little girl stares, transfixed, as a spotted eagle ray (*Aetobatis narinari*) "flies" over her head in an aquatic tunnel. Maui Ocean Center.

The rosy diverticulum of Māʻalaea Bay, with Lānaʻi behind, is dwarfed by celestial radiance.

Though appearing perpetually idyllic, Māʻalaea's beaches become windy after about 11 a.m. each day.

John Severson

One of the fastest, most exciting surfing waves in the world, called "freight train," rises out of Māʻalaea Bay. This break, featured in several movies, looms up when a rare combination of southern storms, offshore winds, and summer swells creates perfect conditions. To stay within its rapidly closing, oval "curl" without falling on the shallow reef requires a fast board and considerable agility.

Bob Hobdy

A radiant dawn from Māʻalaea's pebbly beach.

Early morning at Māʻalaea boat harbor. A US Coast Guard vessel shares space with private and commercial craft. Maui, unlike Oʻahu, has little military activity.

# Maui Ocean Center

Māʻalaea's Maui Ocean Center: The Hawaiian Aquarium states as its mission: "To foster understanding, wonder, and respect for Hawaiʻi's marine life." This three-acre marine park—a remarkable educational facility with 60 self-paced interactive exhibits—showcases only Hawaiian reef, shore, undersea cave, and pelagic (open sea) marine life. Children and adults alike gain a wholesome and exciting perspective on Hawaiʻi's subtropical undersea world, experiencing rare habitats and animals that even professional marine biologists have barely experienced. Its pièce-de-resistance is a 750,000 gallon Open Ocean Exhibit, replete with 2,000 fishes: many sharks, rays, butterfly and damsel fishes, snappers, wrasses, etc., in myriads of species. This gigantic reef and pelagic realm incorporates a 54-foot-long, clear acrylic tunnel through which one can walk in breathtaking proximity to individual fish—especially sharks and rays—as they slide over and around you. Admission rates include discounts for kamaʻāina or Hawaiʻi residents, children, and senior citizens.

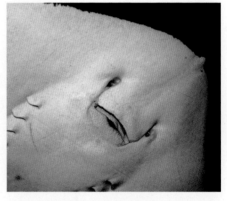

A brown stingray (*Dasyatis latus*), composed primarily of a flat, triangular body—very pale below—flaps gracefully along on enlarged "wings," actually pectoral fins. From below, the "eyes" are actually extra spiracles through which water enters the body to pass over five pairs of gill slits.

Green turtles (*Chelonia mydas*) are Hawai'i's commonest sea turtle, being far more common these days than even 10 years ago. Wild turtles breed primarily in the Northwest Hawaiian Islands National Wildlife Refuge.

A school of blue-lined snapper (*Lutjanus kasmira*) streams past the viewer, just like snorkeling in shallow inshore waters. Turquoise head-to-tail lines contrast with yellowish bodies.

This elegant black-tipped reef shark (*Carcharhinus melanopterus*) is a relatively harmless, common, inshore species. However, it can be aggressive on uninhabited Pacific islands. It is distinguished from other sharks with black-tipped dorsal fins by its relatively short snout.

A highly unusual, fragile exhibit is the Sea Jelly Gallery, where hundreds of transparent jellyfish literally dance before your eyes. Housed in a glorious, floor-to-ceiling acrylic cylinder, one can admire at close range the delicate pumping movements of the jellyfishes' bell-like bodies.

Threadfin or golden butterfly fish (*Chaetodon auriga*) is known as Lau hau in Hawaiian. Commonly seen on reefs, it is easily spotted by its herringbone pattern on yellow and white, plus a threadlike filament extending from its dorsal fin.

The manini or convict tang (*Acanthurus sandvicensis*) is typically the first fish identified by local children or newcomers to the islands. Abundant on shallow inshore reefs, this Hawaiian endemic is named for its black-and-white vertical stripes.

An Indo-Pacific species, this delightful, blue-gray-green oddity, the Unicorn surgeon fish or kala (*Naso brevirostris*) prefers outer reefs or swimmable tunnels and caves around coralheads.

This large spotted, huge-eyed puffer, the porcupinefish or kōkala (*Diodon hystrix*), is harmless as it scoots around coralheads. However, when disturbed, it raises its arsenal of twin-rooted spines and puffs up, presenting an ominous deterrent to potential predators.

Rarely seen in the wild, the fascinating behavior of the peacock flounder or pāki'i (*Bothus mancus*) can be studied with ease. In Lefteye flounders, one eye migrates to the topside during larval development, so that by maturity, both eyes sit adjacent on the left side, an adaptation to camouflaging themselves.

In the museum-like Hawaiians and the Sea Exhibit, a Hawaiian fisherman sits in his dugout outrigger in a lifelike pose. Note the water gourd, "fresh" tuna, a raincoat made from layers of dried ti leaves (*Cordyline fruticosa*). Before paper mulberry (wauke) was introduced to Hawai'i, Hawaiians clothed themselves entirely in garments crafted from ti and banana leaves.

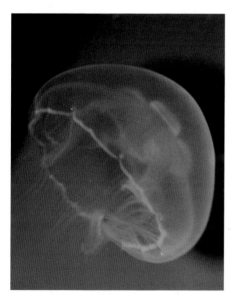 

(left) A single jellyfish, pololia (*Aurelia aurita*) pumps its transparent body gracefully, revealing gossamer tentacles on its periphery and digestive organs inside. (right) A rather busy photo, this one includes a section of coral reef abounding with invertebrates (animals without backbones): orange sea anemones, feathery tubeworms, and multicolored sponges, tunicates, and algae, plus cleaner shrimps.

# Keālia Pond

On the south side of Māʻalaea Bay lies Keālia Pond National Wildlife Refuge, a special home to endangered Hawaiian water birds. In addition, goodly numbers of migratory ducks and shorebirds (spring and fall), plus occasional vagrants such as Ospreys, mainland gulls, etc., surprise birdwatchers and refuge personnel each winter.

(top) Shallow Keālia Pond, whose raised diverticula are crammed with pickleweed (*Batis maritims*), begins a new day. Ten thousand-foot Haleakalā looms against the skyline. (above left) Silvery light highlights Māʻalaea Bay and Keālia Pond from a rainy sky in Olinda. (above right) A 1980 photo from high on Hanaʻula Ridge shows very low water levels. When completely full, the pond swells to 400 acres. (left) A helicopter view of Keālia Pond illustrates its tentative connection to the ocean: Its brackish waters are 1/7 to 1/2 as salty as seawater.

Robert Shallenberger / US Fish & Wildlife Service

A seldom-seen endangered species, the Hawaiian Coot or ʻalae keʻokeʻo, is actually a local subspecies of the American Coot (*Fulica americana alai*). Its statewide numbers are greatest on Maui and Kauaʻi. Coots rarely fly, swim by means of lobed feet (see photo), and build large nests of floating aquatic vegetation. The Hawaiian name means white forehead, referring to the prominent white bill and frontal shield.

The Hawaiian Stilt or aeʻo, a subspecies of the Black-necked Stilt (*Himantopus mexicanus knudseni*) is probably Hawaiʻi's most elegant bird. Tall and slender, this black and white plumaged bird sports brilliant pink legs, which trail during flight. Like the Hawaiian Coot, its major habitats are two ponds on Maui and one on Kauaʻi. Note the adaptive camouflage coloration on both eggs and chick.

# Other Wildlife

Cameron Kepler

Black-crowned Night heron or 'auku'u (*Nycticorax nycticorax hoactli*), a relatively new resident in Hawai'i, is often seen around freshwater and brackish ponds, large and small.

Extremely cute little shorebirds, appearing to "run on wheels," Sanderlings (*Calidris alba*) breed in the Arctic and winter on Hawai'i's sandy shores and salt flats. Their Hawaiian name, huna kai, means sea foam.

US Fish & Wildlife Service

Milkfish or awa (*Chanos chanos*) is a shimmering silvery indigenous fish occurring in Keālia Pond and adjacent aquaculture enclosures. Ancient Hawaiians raised them in walled ponds because of their delicious taste and tolerance of a wide range of salinities.

At Keālia and Kanahā Pond (Kahului) Black-crowned Night herons are common. The crepuscular hours of day are best to see them. Note their jazzy yellow legs and scarlet eyes.

Affectionately known by its Hawaiian name, kōlea, in the Islands, the Pacific Golden-Plover (*Pluvialis fulva*) is a familiar sight, not only at Keālia Pond, but in public parks, private lawns, along coasts, and even high up on Haleakalā. Adults migrate to the Arctic in late spring, raise their young, then return in August, followed miraculously by their new-to-the-world juveniles in late September. (left) Snazzy breeding plumage, developed during April and May. (right top) Nonbreeding plumage and (right bottom) gold spangled dorsal and wing feathers.

Geared to the same annual migratory schedule as the Pacific Golden Plovers, the beautiful black, white, and chestnut Ruddy Turnstones or 'akekeke (*Arenaria interpres*) spend half their year in Hawai'i, the other half—breeding furiously to beat freezing weather and to take advantage of the prolific summer mosquitoes and other tiny flies—in Alaska.

# CHAPTER 5
# McGREGOR POINT TO LAHAINA

Today's modern Pali Road (pron. pah-lee, meaning cliff) skirts the cliff faces for a few miles, gently descending to sea level. Its history is fascinating. The map name, Honoa pi'ilani Highway, derives from the twelfth century. More correctly Hono a Pi'ilani, the name means bays of Pi'ilani. The particular bays (hono in Hawaiian) are six lovely ones north of Kā'anapali, including Honokōwai (a beach park) and Honolua (a surfing mecca). Pi'ilani was either an early chief who ruled these bays or a heavenly maiden who traveled by rainbow from Maui to Lāna'i to visit her lover. The ancient foot trail, widened in the fifteenth century by another Chief Pi'ilani, later bore carriages and cars.

Part of this old carriage trail is now called Lahaina Pali Trail. Dry and hot, it flanks lower Kealaloloa Ridge,

Highway tunnels are rare in Hawai'i. There are two on O'ahu; this, the Pali Tunnel, is the only other public tunnel in the islands.

which includes McGregor Point at its lower, seacliff edge. Begin early with the sun behind you at mile 5 on Route 30 (between the turnoffs to Routes 30 and 310). Take plenty of water and sunscreen, and enjoy the views as you climb to 1,600 feet then down to meet Route 30 again at mile 11 (just past the Pali tunnel). This is not a hike for native plants.

(opposite) The beautiful coastal road—soon to be protected by the Maui Coastal Land Trust as the Pali to Puamana Parkway—closely skirts the ocean, here just north of Papawai Point.

# Whales

Pacific Whale Foundation

Visitors seeking respite from cold climates are not the only winter transients on Maui. Each fall, up to 800 humpback whales also migrate to the Islands and stay until May. Whale watching is a thrilling pastime, and for some a sighting may be an experience that resonates for years. Since whales remain submerged for only eight minutes, on the average, it is usually possible to glimpse the misty spout which signifies that a whale is rising to the surface to expel and inhale air (remember that whales are air-breathing mammals, not fish). Besides the spout, visitors might see a whale's huge black flukes, or a substantial portion of its 35-ton body. The rarest, most breathtaking behavior is a breach, where the whale propels its entire body out of the water, twists, then crashes downward again. Note the humpback's large flippers, largest of all whales, reflected in its scientific name, *Megaptera novaeangliae* (big wing from New England). Check at the resorts for slide shows or videos on whales.

James Hudnall

James Hudnall

These leviathans, sometimes reaching 50 feet in length, have traditionally chosen Maui's sheltered waters for calving. Mothers bear young every two years, after a one-year gestation period. Newborns, 12 feet long, weigh two tons at birth! They grow rapidly on their mother's creamy milk, produced at a rate of 100 to 130 gallons per day.

Scenic lookout (Papawai Point) at mile 8 provides a splendid ocean panorama that includes Māʻalaea Bay, Kahoʻolawe, Lānaʻi and tiny Molokini. From November to May, humpback whales, spouting as close as 50 yards offshore, visit ʻAuʻau Channel, straight ahead. Binoculars are always handy here. Neat, Hawaiian-style rock walls, remains of the original alaloa (a long trail which once skirted the entire island of Maui), can be seen upslope close-by. Several sections of the alaloa are currently being renovated by the State of Hawaiʻi and Sierra Club.

James Hudnall

Humpbacks, like many Maui residents, have two homes: one in the Islands and the other, shown here, in southeast Alaska. In late spring Maui's humpbacks migrate north to the subarctic region, where ocean productivity far exceeds that of the tropics and subtropics. Here their thick insulating blubber allows them to feed and live comfortably in icy waters.

Cameron Kepler

Kīlauea National Wildlife Refuge

Humpback tails are extremely individu-alistic, enabling specific identification of every single whale, a most useful tool for marine mammalogists studying migration and longevity patterns.

Pictured is Aialik Bay, Kenai Fjords National Park in south-central Alaska in late June. Here the humpbacks share protected coves with orcas (killer whales), sea otters, several species of dolphins, the rare Steller's sea lions, and multitudes of breeding seabirds. What a drastic change from life on Maui!

# Coasts & Hills South of Lahaina

Ron Chaple / Blue Hawaiian Helicopters

Closely skirting the gentle ocean, this section of road, from which expansive ocean and mountain vistas can still be enjoyed, is already in the process of new and extensive development. In 1790 Olowalu was the scene of the Olowalu Massacre, a tragic event in Hawai'i's history. As an American fur trading vessel, the *Eleanora*, bartered for fresh food and water from the natives, the ship's lifeboat and its guardian were stolen. Next morning, the furious captain turned out all the native women from his boat, fired at a trading canoe, and burned a small village. He then sailed to nearby Olowalu Village, where he offered handsome rewards for the return of his boat and watchman. They came—after a fashion—as a keel fragment and denuded thighbones. Further enraged, the captain planned a gruesome revenge. He encouraged the trading canoes from Olowalu to visit his ship, then ordered every gun and cannon to be fired, thus killing and wounding hundreds of natives. The sea was awash with blood and flesh. The event was christened Kalolopahu (Slaughter of the Spilled Brains).

Pāpalaua Wayside Park (pron. pah-pah-lah-oo-ah), at mile 11, is representative of the many peaceful beaches—some sandy, some cobbly—that flank Route 30 south of Lahaina. Swim, boogie-board, fish, picnic, or relax here, but beware of underwater rocks and kiawe spines hidden in the sand. Surfers call this beach "Guardrail." Drinking water is not available.

(top) A favorite time for traveling this relatively unmodified stretch of shoreline is dusk, when offshore breezes create feathery rooster tails on the shallow waves, and the sun slips silently behind Lānaʻi. (bottom) Different light vibrations during the day create moods that vary from soothing to glaringly bright. The ubiquitous kiawe (*Prosopis pallida*) trees shed twigs armed with long, sharp spines. Photo taken at Thousand Peaks, a beginner's surfing break.

Ukumehame Canyon, viewed from mile 13, is one of West Maui's most spectacular valleys. Its highest peak (left) sweeps dramatically to a height of 4,457 feet. For centuries, these foothills have been stripped of their original vegetation through the activities of men, cattle, and goats, but the mountains and valleys beyond continue to inspire such visitors as this diarist, one Mr. Gilman: "*It is a scene of rare beauty, particularly at the time of the setting sun when the mountain peaks are in full flush of a coloring which is rarely excelled*." (Thrum's Annual and Almanac 1907).

A helicopter view of Upper Ukumehame Canyon shows the craggy, jumbled terrain typical of West Maui's massif. The shadowed ridge in the middle distance is famous for the daring escape of Chief Kahekili's son during the Battle of Kepaniwai (see Chapter 2). All lands in these two photos—foothills, precipitous valleys, jagged ridges up to the far ridgeline—are now protected. Enormous efforts have been expended to rid this rugged country of feral goats, which stripped vegetation and contributed to severe erosion. The West Maui Forest Reserve & Natural Area Reserve extend from Pāpalaua Gulch to Launiupoko Stream.

Agriculture and tourism are Maui's major industries. Sugar, a lowland crop, covers more than 47,000 acres on the island, 185,000 acres statewide. Botanically a tall grass, sugar is planted as stem cuttings, watered plentifully, burned to remove organic debris, and harvested over a two-year period. One ton of water is required to produce one pound of sugar, so it is no wonder that most of West Maui's streams, tapped for irrigation, rarely reach the ocean. During the nineteenth century and early twentieth century, Asian laborers were imported to the Islands to assist the sugar industry. Pay was poor and plantation life very regimented. Due to overwork, miserable living conditions, and unfair treatment by their superiors, workers periodically organized strikes. Thousands pleaded to be sent home, and many did return to their homelands as soon as their

contracts expired. Cane-field labor was, and still is a hot, dusty, 14-hour-a-day job. Around 1900, a Japanese laborer earned $12 a month. Of this, it is said, $11 was sent to his family in Japan. Today, sugar is no longer "king" on West Maui, since Lahaina's Pioneer Mill recently closed.

A fisherman tries his luck at trapping small reef fish in the rocky shallows along Route 30. His circular nylon net is weighted along the edge with smooth stones. Before throwing the net, the fisherman pleats it carefully, then with lightning speed tosses it upward and outward. This traditional fishing technique is a picturesque reminder of life in old Hawai'i, although today the rewards are meager. Early Hawaiians used numerous methods, individual and cooperative, to capture fish. Authentic nets, some of which are displayed in the Bishop Museum, Honolulu, were manufactured from fine threads of olonā, a native nettle with strong fibers. A stain extracted from burnt kukui nuts helped prolong the net's life.

(left) From mile 14 to 16 are scattered beaches beside shallows enclosed by a barrier reef. These are good for novice snorkelers. (right) View toward Haleakalā from a beach near the surfing spot locally dubbed Thousand Peaks.

Launiupoko State Wayside Park, (pron. low (rhymes with cow)-nee-oo-po-ko), at mile 18, with silvery sand, is spacious and restful. Its six acres of lawns, beach, coconut palms, and picnic facilities include water, an outdoor shower, and a relative rarity on Maui, public toilets. Its verdant character today stands in sharp contrast to its desolate nature two centuries ago.

Inland of the coast and lower foothills, West Maui's valleys change character markedly. Pictured here is waterfall at Launiupoko Valley, a few miles inland from the sunny beach park.

A distant view of Launiupoko Beach Area from way up-valley. On the left is Līhau Peak, 4,197 feet.

Olowalu Valley—all West Maui's valleys are vital sources of fresh water and will become even more so now that (as of 2005) an extra 45,000 residents are planned for this general area.

# CHAPTER 6 LAHAINA

Lahaina (pron. la-high-nah), because of its geographic location, has long been a town dedicated to frivolity: a surfing and loafing "resort" for Hawaiian royalty; a lascivious playground for raunchy sailors; and, more recently, a surfing, loafing, shopping, pleasure-centered resort for international vacationers. The town's essential spirit still survives.

Lahaina is also rich in history, not only that of Maui but of the entire state. Since approximately 1100, the Lahaina–Kā'anapali area has hosted noble families. It was the royal capital of the Islands from 1802 to 1854, when Hawaiian royalty coexisted—not always peacefully—with lusty whalers and stern missionaries. In the latter half of the nineteenth century, Asian laborers, imported to toil on the sugar plantations, added distinctive cultural overlays. Because of the decline in whaling, by 1900 Lahaina had become a deserted village devoid of hotels. Today, East and West, old and new, mingle uniquely.

Lahaina (population 9,000) though only a few blocks long, is rich with remnants of past eras, thanks to the Lahaina Restoration Foundation, which, in the early 1960s, began the enormous task of restoring the town's historic sites. Lahaina has been a National Historic Landmark since 1964. Street maps are in all free publications including the small booklet *Lahaina Historical Guide*, to which the historic site numbers in this book refer.

Within Lahaina's limited boundaries the shopper may find a sensational assortment of both imported and Island-made goods, ranging from the elegant to the vulgar, including art, clothing, jewelry, ornaments, and food. Start early, armed with sunglasses, or you might wilt in the noonday heat. To reach Lahaina, turn onto Front Street from Route 30 at mile 19.

Lahaina's few beaches are private with obscure rights-of-way or none at all. Their waters are shallow and permeated with sharp corals. Kā'anapali's golden strands are somewhat more accessible, although public parking is restricted.

(opposite) A 12-foot high Buddha, a replica of the noted statue in Kamakura, Japan (45 feet high, dated A.D. 1252), was unveiled in 1968 to commemorate Japanese migration to Hawai'i. Cameron Kepler

Lahaina's famous Indian banyan tree (*Ficus benghalensis*) is the hub of town. Park your car (if you can) and shop, visit historic sites, or explore the colorful harbor. Banyans, characterized by curious dangling aerial roots and multiple trunks, are common in Hawai'i. This one (Historic Site No. 9 on Front Street near the Pioneer Inn) is of particular interest. Planted in 1873 to honor the 50th anniversary of the first Protestant missionaries, it is one of the world's largest banyans. Now 50 feet high, it stretches across more than 200 feet and covers two-thirds of an acre. In a town whose name means "merciless sun," such extensive shade, complete with seats, is certainly welcome. A National Historic Landmark, this tree is fastidiously nurtured and shaped; please discourage children from playing on it. The name banyan was originally applied to Hindu merchants who spread their wares beneath such trees. How appropriate that every Saturday, Maui artists also display and sell items—paintings, photographs, sculptures—right at this location.

(opposite) Picturesque Lahaina Harbor is jam-packed with private and commercial boats. Charters are available for whale watching or reef-viewing, sport fishing, snorkel/scuba tours to Lāna'i and Molokini, and sunset cruises. Turn makai (seaward) of the banyan tree on Front Street. James Michener, author of the epic novel *Hawai'i*, once listed among his eight most cherished sights: No. 1, snow on the Big Island volcanoes, and No. 2, the small boats returning to shore as dusk falls on Lahaina.

Bob Abraham

Bishop Museum Archives

A landmark of Lahaina, the Pioneer Inn (Historic Site No. 8) is centrally located on the waterfront north of the banyan tree. Although first built in 1901, too late to lodge whalers (who left 40 years earlier), the inn's present nineteenth century ambience and whaling memorabilia evoke a time when Lahaina's streets teemed with pleasure-seeking sailors. The original house rules included the following admonitions: "Women is not allowed in you room" and "If you wet or burn you bed you going out." The Pioneer Inn, whose popularity has not diminished since those times, still contributes heartily to Lahaina's nightlife. Lower photo depicts the inn circa 1915.

A glistening pacific blue marlin (*Makaira nigricans*) comes ashore. Clothed in shiny metallic-blue with vertical stripes, this pelagic marlin is the most common billfish caught in Hawai'i, inhabiting surface waters of the open sea, along with 'ahi (yellowfin tuna) and the famous mahimahi (dolphin fish). To try your luck in Hawai'i, the Billfish Capital of the World, charter boats are available from Mā'alaea, Lahaina, or Kona (island of Hawai'i). Summer months are best, no license is necessary, and boats supply everything. Most charters keep the bulk of daily catches, so if you want more than one night's dinner, filleted by the crew, make arrangements beforehand. On Maui, average marlin weights run 200–300 pounds. In 1986, an 874-pound black marlin (*Makaira indica*), winner of the Lahaina Jackpot, was the third largest billfish

ever caught on Maui. An increasing number of boats and fishermen these days practice catch-and-release in deference to conservation of the seas' diminishing resources.

**Pioneer Inn, viewed through the famous banyan tree.**

Seaward of the harbor lie the open Lahaina Roadsteads, whose easy access and relatively shallow, calm waters are suitable for pleasure boats—that is, until Maui's annual winter storms whip through. Between 1820 and 1870, this area was the prime Pacific anchorage of the American whaling fleet. When whaling was at its peak, an 1846 census of Lahaina listed 429 whale ships, 882 grass houses, 115 adobe huts, 59 dwellings of wood or stone, and 3,557 people.

(top) For those who have spent time at sea—within sight of land or amid a vast ocean far from habitation—the sight of boats reflected in calm waters and the salty breeze mingle to stir one's inner nautical longings. (bottom) Whisking along in a mild breeze off Lahaina Roadsteads is a replica of a Hawaiian double-hulled canoe with a traditional crab claw sail. Unfortunately few details are known about ancient Hawaiian double canoes. Early Western visitors to the Islands—explorers, missionaries, and whalers—remarked casually that huge double canoes reached 60, 75, or 90 feet in length, but measurements are few. However, details of the elaborate rituals, omens, and spiritual preparation which attended canoe-making are better known.

Douglas Peebles

Cameron Kepler

Typical of seaports anywhere, Lahaina has its share of colorful sea captains. Cheery, weather-beaten faces pop up everywhere—from the Pioneer Inn's porch (left) or a catamaran houseboat (right).

Bishop Museum Archives / Baker Collection

A Hawaiian lady mends fishing nets in Lahaina around 1912. Note the traditional woven mats and Mother Hubbard mu'umu'u, a legacy from the missionaries.

David Davis

Today a shopper's delight, Front Street is one of the oldest and most historical thoroughfares in Hawai'i. Though modernized, it retains a distinctly nineteenth century architectural style, due in part to its renovation for the movie "Hawai'i."

Nakamoto Art Studio

Front Street early this century. Soon after this photo was taken, a seawall was built to protect the road from winter storms. During the time of royal residency (sixteenth to nineteenth century), Front Street was called Alanui Mō'ī or King's Road.

A bird's-eye view of Lahaina with the West mountains in the background. Douglas Peebles

This ancient art of etching miniature pictures into ivory, shell, and bone, was practiced independently by American Indians, Polynesians, Eskimos, and bored sailors everywhere. Waiting lovers, fantasies, and maritime topics remain its primary themes. During the grand whaling era, scrimshanders used nails for outlining, sail needles or jack knives for carving, small chisels for inlaying, lamp black for staining, sharkskin for smoothing, and sailmaker's wax for polishing. Although modern scrimshaw is highly professional, old pieces, many valuable, carry a high sentimental value. Life at sea was bitterly hard—food and pay were miserable, the stench of dead whales was nauseating, and sickness was common. After years of hard work, most sailors had little more than a few souvenirs, a weak body, ragged clothes, and some hand-carved whale's teeth. Lahaina is today a world center for scrimshaw; products range from tiny charms to heirloom investments. Since 1973, when the importation of whale products to the United States was banned, fossil ivory has become a favored medium for engravings. Some walrus teeth are 2,000 years old, while mastodon tusks extend back 50,000 years. Martin Bandy's work (above) is noted for its intricate details conveying facial expressions, postures, and moods.

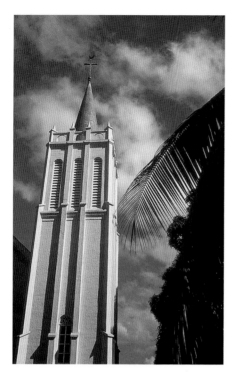

Maria Lanakila Church, Historic Site No. 26, the oldest Catholic church on Maui, is a concrete replica of a wooden house of worship erected in 1828. It is located at the corner of Waine'e and Dickenson streets. The first Catholic priest arrived on Maui in 1846, much to the consternation of the Protestant missionaries who thought they were doing a fine job of converting the "heathen" to their own faith. During the next few decades, thousands of Portuguese and Filipino Catholics arrived, swelling the numbers of Catholic converts. Today, Catholicism is the largest Christian denomination in the state.

*"'This is beastly!' I heard one man remark as he climbed out of his berth. 'Wake up at one o'clock in the morning to go ashore, and not find a single hotel where one can get accommodation,'"* so complained an 1890s traveler to Lahaina who was visiting various spots on Maui via steamer vessel (*in Hawai'i...Our New Possessions* by J. R. Musick 1898). Today's situation is greatly improved, although Lahaina has limited accommodations compared to Kā'anapali and resorts further north. Today no visitor needs to worry about finding accommodations or their quality.

Pierre of Lahaina Studios / Lahaina Restoration Foundation

Baldwin Home, a residence of the Reverend and Mrs. Dwight Baldwin from 1838 to 1871, is now a delightfully authentic museum. This stately family home, donated to Maui by family heirs, pays homage to all missionaries in Hawai'i. It is centrally located on a shady corner of Front Street near the banyan tree.

On display are paintings, family treasures, period furniture, an antiquated medical kit, a piano with hymnbook (right), and everyday articles. A busy missionary and physician, Baldwin was also intimately involved in community affairs. He was a primary force in controlling the "sinful" antics of whalers and in educating the "natives" in practical and religious matters. As befitted his community position, he also hosted Hawaiian royalty, visiting dignitaries, and ship captains. In Hawai'i, the Baldwin name is synonymous with missionaries and success. Beginning with Baldwin's own six children, the family's descendants have become prominent in Island business, agriculture, ranching, commerce, tourism, and philanthropy. The Alexander and Baldwin Company is so well known it is listed in the phone directory as A&B!

(opposite) A memorable sunset offshore Lahaina with exceptionally calm seas.

By 1852, lawlessness had grown to such a degree that the Old Fort (below) was sorely inadequate. Using coral blocks stripped from the fort, prisoners built a high wall around a small wooden structure (above), the old prison, Hale Pa'ahao (House Stuck in Irons). Offenses leading to imprisonment included ship desertion, drunkenness, and dangerous horse riding. Fines were stiff. For example, a list from 1844 runs thus: $10 for "lewd, seductive and lascivious conduct," $50 for rape, $6 for "desecrating the Sabbath," and $10 for "coming ashore with a knife, sword cane or any other dangerous weapon." Relative to salaries, such prices for misconduct were exorbitant. For four years' work, a captain received the grand sum of $380, while at the lower end of the scale, a cabin boy pocketed a mere $28.

The Old Fort (Historic Site No. 11), on the waterfront, is an authentic-looking 1960s reconstruction of a fort that existed between 1832 and the 1850s. Composed of coral blocks hewn from the nearby reef, it was 20 feet high and enclosed one acre of ground. The fort was built by royal command during the whaling era when unruly behavior was rife. At one time, 47 cannons sat atop its walls. The original fort was disassembled to construct a larger compound, the Old Prison (above).

If it were not for the lusty whalers, this little town would not have needed all its prisons, forts, stiff rules, and punishments. Notice, though, that the whales in the painting are sperm whales (a type of toothed whale), which were the raison d'etre of the whaling industry. Sperm whales are cold-water species, most common off Japan. Hawai'i's humpback whales were only a small part of the whaling industry, and even though Lahaina had a few shore-based whaling stations, humpbacks were rarely taken.

(left) The remains of Lahaina's Old Fort guard the south corner of Canal Street, makai of the banyan tree. (right) The court house, next to the fort, faces the harbor. It was built in 1859 to house a court, a jury room, and government and customs offices. An earlier, tin-roofed building had been destroyed by furious winds whipping from the north coast, over West Maui's topmost ridges, and down Kaua'ula Valley (the valley directly behind Lahaina) to Lahaina town. Such destructive weather is most unusual; normally Lahaina is calm and hot, except for occasional winter storms from the south.

# Wo Hing Temple

The first Chinese immigrants came to Hawai'i as sandalwood merchants around 1800, well before the missionaries and whalers. Fifty years later, larger waves of Chinese were imported as sugar plantation laborers. The Wo Hing Temple, Historic Site No. 29, originally built in 1912 and fastidiously renovated in 1983, is a fascinating museum. It is located just north of the junction of Front Street and Lahainaluna Road. Today Maui has an extremely small Chinese population compared to O'ahu. Japanese (20%), Hawaiian and part-Hawaiian (26%), haole or Caucasians (25%) and Filipinos (16%) are the major ethnic groups.

**(left) Twenty feet away from bustling, tourist-oriented Front Street, a calm room is dominated by an orchid-decorated Buddha. Hanging lanterns (right), a metallic candle (below), and numerous artifacts—all so Chinese. Is this Lahaina?**

(left) A corner of the Wo Hing Temple's Chinese kitchen. (right) Buddha, holding a lotus symbol of enlightenment, is an important figure to Asians.

(right) An old, zither-like Chinese musical instrument. (below) Many miles of irrigation ditches and tunnels honeycomb West Maui's rugged mountains. Most were hand-chipped out of solid rock by Chinese laborers. They skirt deep ravines and precipitous cliffs, serving as monuments to these early immigrants who helped weave Hawai'i's present cultural, social, and agricultural fabric. Photo shows the author, with headlamp, emerging from a long water tunnel high above Honokōhau Valley.

# Lahaina Jodo Mission Cultural Park

The meticulously tended Lahaina Jodo Mission Cultural Park houses Gautama Buddha (above and below), flanked by a scarlet fruiting Manila palm (*Veitchia merrillii*) and summer flowering rainbow shower tree (*Cassia X nealii*). The pagoda safeguards ashes of the dead.

(left) During summer, a colorful event is the bon dance featuring taiko drums and dancers dressed in kimonos. A special ceremony involves hundreds of tiny "candle boats" floating out to sea at sunset, lighting the journey of souls to Nirvana, the land of bliss. Further ceremonies and dances honor Buddha's birthday in early April at all Buddhist temples in the state. (right) A close-up view of the Pagoda's intricate woodwork. If it were not for the coconut palm and rainbow shower tree, both tropical, one might think this photo was taken in Japan.

(left) An elaborately painted ceiling and flower-decked altar adorn the Japanese temple. (right) Across the road from the mission park sits a cemetery within the sand dunes.

# Mosquitoes & Miscellaneous Topics

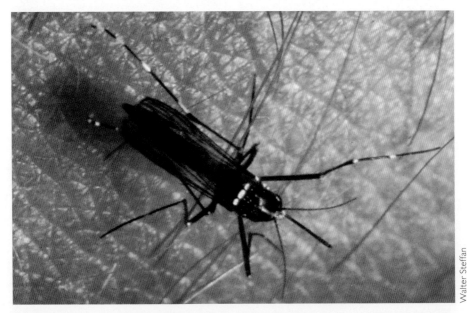

Walter Steffan

Mosquitoes, the pesky little insects that inhabit Hawai'i from sea level to around 3,500 feet elevation, may be appropriately mentioned here. In 1826, the crew of the whaling ship *Wellington*, returning to Lahaina to hunt women and alcohol, confronted new laws of fines for misdemeanors. According to the Hawaiian chief and missionaries, there were to be no grog shops, no brothels and not even any women swimming out to the ships! Enraged, the sailors emptied a water cask, last filled in Mexico, into a freshwater stream. Within this cask lived larvae of mosquitoes (*Culex quinquefasciatus*). From that fateful date, mosquitoes have bitten every resident and visitor to the Hawaiian Islands. There are now five species of mosquitoes in Hawai'i that bite humans, none of which transmit diseases. However, they do carry avian malaria, a disease similar to human malaria, that is lethal to birds. This has played such havoc with Hawai'i's native bird populations that, along with forest destruction and introduced mammals, 20 percent of the world's extinct birds were from Hawai'i.

Embarking into new floral territory, armed with a dizzying selection of tropical flowers, new breeds of artists have emerged. Sometimes, they bow to the traditional *ikebana* style. Sometimes they soar on individual flights of floral fancy. Regardless, there is always balance, whether *shin* (core), *soe* (auxiliary), and *tai* (body), providing a basic triangle of differing lengths or a more Western-style equilibrium.

Traditional Japanese flower arranging or *ikebana* thrives throughout Maui, but especially in the older residential areas of Lahaina, Kahului, and Wailuku. Generally associated with Buddhist church groups, it is mostly taught and practiced by those who immigrated from Japan decades ago. Photo shows white chrysanthemums (symbol of October) and local Christmas berry. Ikebana's underlying philosophy is based on a love for and respect of nature.

Another Japanese custom greets you at almost every doorstep in Hawai'i; Island residents are horrified when you walk into their houses with shoes on! Incidentally, locals call flip-flops "slippers."

(above) This very early, undated photo, entitled "Lagoon-Marsh, Lahaina," shows one of the many lakes, marshes, and streams which enriched Lahaina's shoreline before the advent of sugar agribusiness. The tranquil street scene (below) is also undated.

In 1831, Lahainaluna High School, the first high school west of the Rockies, was founded. Its first students were Hawaiian, and all instruction and textbooks were in Hawaiian. In addition to studying, the pupil's activities included farming, phoneticizing the Hawaiian language, compiling Hawaiian dictionaries, and operating Maui's first printing press. This respected school still emphasizes Hawaiian culture. Its grounds are shaded with mature trees, including an elegant entryway of royal palms. David Malo Day, honoring an early Hawaiian scholar, is celebrated each spring. To reach the school, turn north at the sugar mill at mile 20 on Route 30. The large white "L" on the hill behind Lahaina represents Lahainaluna and is limed twice a year by students.

# Lahaina's Flowers & Fruits

Lahaina is ablaze with color, especially during summer. These pages show trees that are particularly common in Lahaina. Brilliant partners, allamanda flowers (*Allamanda cathartica*) and croton leaves (*Codiaeum variegatum*) have long beautified Island gardens, thriving in bright sunshine.

The light papery seedpods of the African tulip tree (above) are occasionally fashioned into unusual lei.

African Tulip trees (*Spathodea campanulata*), along with plumerias, palms, and assorted tropical ornamentals, can be seen in the Lahaina–Kāʻanapali area. These dark-foliaged trees also mingle with lush lowland foliage along the Hāna Highway. Year-round clusters of brilliant "tulips" characterize this handsome tree which is easily recognizable from a distance. Native to tropical Africa and unrelated to true tulips, the dazzling orange flowers resemble lopsided originals from Holland.

Unknown in the wild state, lychees (*Litchi chinensis*), native to southern China and cultivated for more than 2,000 years in Asia, were introduced to Hawai'i in 1873 by Chinese immigrants. To fruit abundantly, lychee trees need full sun, ample water, and wind protection, conditions met in Lahaina. When they are in season (summer), the trees literally droop with generous clusters of crimson, rough-skinned (almost prickly) fruit, during which time they are usually available in supermarkets. Inside their thin shell lies a deliciously sweet, white-translucent, juicy pulp, reminiscent of grapes in texture and flavor.

An 1820s prediction for Lahaina by resident C. S. Stewart has come true: *"The taste, skill and industry of an American gardener might convert it into an earthly Paradise; but now every where (sic) appears only like the neglected grounds of a deserted plantation."* One of Lahaina's most common trees today, shading even the smallest backyards, is the mango (*Mangifera indica*). Lahaina's "merciless sun" ripens its fruits into super-sweet, orange, finger-licking delectables, not to be missed from May to July. Varieties Haden and Pirie are best.

(left) The best papayas in the world—with no exceptions—are those ripened on the tree. Lahaina is an excellent place to grow them, since they rarely develop fungus diseases there, a condition which besets plants in more humid areas. Papayas need excellent drainage, plenty of fertilizer, and ample water, especially when young. Maui wisdom dictates that "papayas like wet toes but not wet feet." Many varieties are available; pictured is a relatively new hybrid Exotica, with one parent, the Hawaiian Solo.

(top, left) Pineapples (*Ananas comosus*), with hula girls, coconuts, and hibiscus as allies, virtually epitomize Hawai'i. However, these delectable fruits MUST be field-ripened; after picking, they no longer produce any sugar. Pineapples are bromeliads, originating in tropical America. Their tiny purple flowers bear large fleshy ovaried which eventually coalesce to form a collective fruit.

New hybrids such as Sugarloaf (left) are so mesmerizingly sweet, they literally melt in your mouth. Fruits are easy to grow (just plant the dried-out leaf crown), take at least 1-1/2 years to mature, and need ample iron, fertilizer, and water.

(left, bottom) A young pineapple still with its tiny purple flowers.

(above) From South Africa, the Natal plum (*Carissa macrocarpa*) makes a good, ever-blooming spiny hedge which, as an added bonus, produces scarlet, plum-like fruits which simmer into a delicious ice cream topping-cum-jam.

A fairly popular banana cultivar, the Dwarf Red doubles as an ornamental. Its bright red trunks bear fruits, which vary from chocolate (young), pink-and-green to maroon. The fruits are very tasty when both semi-ripe and fully ripe.

There's nothing like the thought of yellow passionfruit (*Passiflora edulis flava*) to inspire one's stomach juices to flow. They grow rampantly in Lahaina's climate. The flowers (left) illustrate elements of the Catholic Easter Passion (that's all!). For a novelty, spoon the pulp out like eating a boiled egg (right).

Ua ka ua,
ola ka nohonao ka ʻāina kula

*The rain pours,
life comes to the plains.*

—Ancient Hawaiian wisdom

If Lahaina and Kāʻanapali are scorching hot and dry, the opposite is true of the verdant mountains visible from their shores. Only a few miles inland from the popular beaches lies a world of fabulous cascades, dripping mossy forests, and soggy bogs harboring an impressive list of 127 plant ecosystem types, 30 of which are found nowhere else on earth. Largely inaccessible, here lie fragile ecosystems where daily rain feeds numerous waterfalls which plunge more than 1,000 dizzying feet into deep ravines. Early travelers raved over their beauty: "[The mountains were] rocky and precipitous, torn by deep shadowy ravines and cavernous gorges. Many who have traveled extensively for the sake of observing natural scenery declare they have never seen mountains which in variety and form, coloring and beauty, exceed the mountains of Maui" (*Hawaiʻi... Our New Possessions*, 1898, by John Musick).

West Maui's interior massif is scarcely a range of mountains in the accepted sense. It more resembles an irregular circle of steep valleys and knife-edged ridges radiating, like wheel spokes, from several central boggy flats. Puʻu Kukui, 5,788 feet high and West Maui's highest point, is also not a true peak but the topmost bog on a spectacular cloud-hugging ridge which forms the mountain's "backbone."

Two reasons why these mountains and valleys are so verdant and sharply precipitous are because they are geologically very young (1.3 million years old) and they receive copious rain. Heavy rainfall also means that when the vegetative cover is disturbed or removed, serious erosion takes place causing silty runoff which kills the offshore coral reefs. Vital subterranean and surface water reserves then become severely depleted.

In former times, Hawaiians treasured their upland watersheds; wao akua, a spirit inhabited wilderness, was a sacred home of the living forest, together with its flora and fauna. On West Maui, life-giving waters flowing downward to inhabited areas irrigated taro and other food crops. Herbs for

**(opposite) A giant, bog-loving lobelia, ʻōpelu (*Lobelia gloria-montis*) is indeed a "glory of the mountain." This endemic Hawaiian beauty favors high bogs and their dwarfed forest margins (4,500–5,800 feet).** Pat Bily

medicines, woods for carving, fibers for cordage, and feathers for featherwork were harvested judiciously. In the late 1800s, with the advent of sugar production, massive ecological changes to the lower forests occurred, including large-scale stream diversions. However, since 1890, genuine concern for the health of these rugged, cloud-capped watershed lands—a vital ecological reserve—has resulted in various partnerships of state and private landowners.

The latest, most comprehensive coalition, formed in 1998 and covering more than 50,000 acres of ridges, slopes, and summits, is the West Maui Mountains Watershed Partnership. Its principal partners—AMFAC/JMB Hawaii; C. Brewer & Co.; Hawai'i State Department of Natural Resources; Kamehameha Schools; Maui County; Maui Land & Pineapple Company; and The Nature Conservancy of Hawai'i—are unanimously devoted to the management priorities of controlling destructive feral mammals (goats, pigs, deer, cattle) and invasive weeds, promoting public education and activities, and monitoring water/watershed.

Prime—albeit disjunct—land parcels include four state-owned West Maui Natural Area Reserves (Kahakuloa, Honokōwai, Pana'ewa, Līhau, totaling 6,702 acres), nine West Maui State Forest Reserves, The Nature Conservancy's Kapunakea Reserve (1,200 acres), AMFAC/JMB lands (Olowalu, Ukumehame, Kaua'ula, Launiupoko, Helu, Kapunakea) and Pu'u Kukui Watershed Management Area (8,600 acres).

Esthetically, we might also add that the sheer geological and ecological beauty of the West Maui massif—its spectacular volcanic scenery and plethora of native plants and animals (many found nowhere else in the world)—is worth preserving for its own sake. A few areas still remain as pristine as centuries ago...rare fragments of Hawai'i's 'āina, the sacred land.

'Eke Crater, a lone summit bog, rises to 4480 feet almost dead center of the West Maui massif. A northward view from upper Honokōhau Valley.

Everyone has heard of Maui's famous Haleakalā silversword on East Maui, but few are aware of its West Maui counterpart, the 'eke silversword (*Argyroxiphium calignis*). This stunning, silvery dwarf stands only about 1½ feet tall.

Aerial, Kaho'olewa Ridge, snaking through the central massif, separating watersheds east and west. 'Eke Crater lies at distant left. This is all very fragile country; although 70 percent of the West Maui watershed maintains native vegetation cover, much of it is highly vulnerable to erosional disturbance by feral mammals.

A biologist trudges up yet another ridge from base camp to 'Eke Crater. To the left the upper reaches of Kahakuloa Stream drop sharply.

Strangely, Maui's spectacular greensword (*Argyroxiphium grayanum*), restricted to high summit bogs, has no Hawaiian name. Closely related to silverswords, it lacks silvery leaves, an adaptation to a wetter substrate.

(left) Clusters of fragile greensword (*Argyroxiphium grayanum*) rosettes huddle among bog-side vegetation near Puʻu Kukui, West Maui's highest point (5,788 feet). (right) A loosely packed flower cluster reveals its taxonomic home in the daisy family (Compositae).

(left) Young greenswords carpet a wide boggy ridge high above world-famous surfing spot, Honolua Bay. (right) A pristine bog, with stalked ʻōpelu (*Lobelia gloria-montis*), dwarfed ʻōhiʻa (*Metrosideros polymorpha*), sporting a single red pompon, and uluhe fern (*Dicranopteris linearis*).

Pat Bily

Pā makani (*Viola maviensis*), one of Hawai'i's 11 species of endemic, rarely seen violets. They likely originated on Alaska's Arctic tundra, their seeds accidentally traveling to Hawai'i lodged between the toes of the migratory kōlea (Lesser Golden-Plovers).

(left) A tiny, rare, daisy, hōwaiaulu (*Lagenifera maviensis*), another Maui endemic, is restricted to high elevation bogs. Its rosette form indicates that it, along with the violet (above), and common sundew (right), "flew" from the Arctic to Hawai'i embedded in mud on golden plover feet. Indeed, it is identical to the great sundew, a long-leaf, very "northern" species. Hawaiians were familiar with this unusual insect-catcher (*Drosera anglica*), naming it mikinalo.

How wondrous! The candelabra form of giant lobelia or ʻōpelu (*Lobelia gloria-montis*), emerging from ever-present mists clothing West Maui's summits.

(left) Mature, dwarfed ʻōhiʻa "trees" (*Metrosideros polymorpha subsp. polymorpha, form humilis var. pseudorugosa*) in bogs are so tiny, they may only attain 4–5 inches! Ancient names include "flattened-," "creeping-," "misty face-," "spreading lehua," and "wind creeper." (right) Emerging from a matted bog; ʻōpelu curves outward its long spikes of purple and white blossoms.

(left) Carpeted with thick dripping mosses, these dwarf fairylands bathe in nearly constant fog. In these moist spongy nurseries, ferns, saplings, and vines all vie for space. Ferns attain their greatest numbers, diversity, and beauty in wet montane forests. (right top) Hawai'i's endemic wahine no mauna (lady of the mountains), *Adenophorus pinnatifidus* and (right bottom) palai hihi (creeping palai), *Vandenboschia davalloides*. Hawai'i harbors 188 species and varieties of native ferns, fully 14 percent of all native plants.

Top-of-the-world Violet Lake, 5,000 feet above Lahaina, enjoys a blink of sun (left) in contrast to its usual shrouding clouds (right).

# Upper Montane Forests

Hawai'i's endemic red hibiscus, koki'o 'ula'ula (*Hibiscus kokio ssp. kokio*) is a rare treasure, even in Kapunakea Preserve. Found on all main islands, and variable in shape and color, its petals are squarish and silky to the touch.

(above and below) The upper reaches of Honokōwai Valley support diverse moist and wet native rain forests. Its cloud-cloaked headwaters originate on West Maui's highest and wettest location, Pu'u Kukui (5788 feet).

The yellow form of 'ōhi'a lehua (*Metrosideros polymorpha*), was named lehua mamo.

One of my favorites, this hāhā (*Cyanea macrostegia atra*) is palm-like, with long coarse leaves and astounding stiff, purple-black, curved, knobby flowers. Rare, it is threatened by the ravages of cattle and pigs.

Chris Brosius / WMMWP

Chris Brosius / WMMWP

Cameron Kepler

(above left) 'Ohe mauka (*Tetra-plasandra oahuense*) is related to a common houseplant, the octopus or umbrella tree (*Schefflera actinophylla*). Favoring wet to moist forests, mature trees may reach 30 feet tall. The beautiful magenta flowers shown here are one inch across. (above right) A rare native Hawaiian land snail (*Succinea sp*), characterized by scoop-like, paper-thin shells. (left) Primitive *Partulinas* spawned tremendous diversity in the famous *Achatinella* snails. This rare, stripy species may be *P. splendida*, a West Maui endemic.

A hiker's view of the fabulous, double-tiered Honokōhau Falls, 1,120 feet high, is the loftiest perennial, named waterfall on Maui. It presides over West Maui's heart at the head of Honokōhau Valley.

(above and below) Cerise, curved flowers adorn the multibranching koliʻi (*Trematolobelia macrostachys*), a denizen of high elevation forest edge and bogs. There is no easy way to reach these forests; hikers may inquire about Sierra Club Service trips. All Hawaiʻi's lobelias are adapted for pollination by Hawaiʻi's endemic honeycreepers, which are nectar feeders with curved beaks.

Betsy Gagné

An unusual, fragrant native plant, hōʻawa (*Pittosporum confertifolum*), highlights the Waiheʻe Ridge Trail.

The elegant bird's nest fern or ʻēkaha (*Asplenium nidus*) tolerates a wide range of ecological conditions. Here it perches on a dry rock face, upper Launiupoko Valley. Its parallel brown spore patterns mark it as an Asplenium. This large epiphytic fern occurs throughout the Pacific.

Hoi kuahiwi (*Smilax melastomifolia*) snakes across a lacy tree fern frond (*hāpuʻu, Cibotium glaucum*).

Fortunately this is not a rare endemic plant, and can be found in all of Maui's montane forests. The ʻieʻie (*Freycinetia arborea*), a climbing pandanus, is simply a small, viney, twining hala (*Pandanus tectorius*). Watch for its deep salmon bracts and pollen-laden flowers from spring to fall.

Today restricted to West Maui summits, this striking ʻōhā wai (*Clermontia micrantha*) is stalked with curved, rosy flowers crowded inside the rosette leaf crown. Another pretty rare endemic.

Hank Oppenheimer

(above and right) Nuku'i'iwi (*Strongylodon ruber*), named for the beak of the dazzling scarlet endemic 'i'iwi honeycreeper. One of the few plants cultivated by Hawaiians for its lei flowers, tradition warns us not to pick or wear the flowers if we do not respect the ancient gods.

*"The 'i'iwi is there*
*High in the forest canopy*
*Dipping its curved beak*
*Deep into the red lehua blossom.*
*The Nuku 'i'iwi is there*
*High in the forest canopy*
*Thrusting its blooms earthward*
*Majestic ornaments*
*Desired lei for royal beings."*

Ron Nagata

The steep ridges of striking Ukumehame Valley are clearly etched in late afternoon light. This photo was taken during an aerial flight to Kahului, Maui, from the Island of Hawai'i.

(left) An extremely rare native mint, *Phyllostegia stachyoides*, blooming amid a tapestry of ferns, orchids, and other delicate understory plants. Areas supporting such floral gems have been severely depleted over the years by unrestrained cattle. (right) A vale of enormous circular leaves of 'ape'ape (*Gunnera petaloidea*) identify a strange, little-known family dating back more than 50 million years. A typical leaf is three feet in diameter.

John Carothers

(left) A tiny native twayblade or 'awapuhiakanaloa (*Liparis hawaiensis*), one of Hawai'i's three endemic orchid species. It is very similar to several species in Southeast Asia, from whence its miniscule seeds likely drifted in high jet streams. All Hawai'i's splashy orchids are introduced from Asia or tropical America. (right) Another rare endemic mint, *Stenogyne kamehamehae*. Although in the mint family, this vine is non-aromatic.

# Feral Mammals

David Boynton

The only tropical rain forest in the United States grow in the far-flung islands of Hawai'i. Here, native plants, which evolved over several million years, are so unique that 90 percent of the species are not found anywhere else in the world (i.e., they are endemic). Feral pigs (*Sus scrofa*), a Polynesian-European mixed breed, have generated such severe damage to the precious forests and watersheds that today millions of dollars are spent controlling their ever-expanding populations.

Cameron Kepler

Extreme pig damage to forest, resulting in masses of subsurface roots and no soil.

Alan Holt / The Nature Conservancy

A brown, soil exposed 'Eke Crater is the result of pig rootings and subsequent erosion.

Alan Holt / The Nature Conservancy

Fencing out pigs from forests is standard procedure in Hawai'i these days.

Beach debris resulting from pig disturbance of East Maui's forest understory and subsequent erosion back and forth into the ocean.

(left) Feral cattle—who do not always respect fences—plough through delicate forests, literally like "bulls in china shops." (right) This damage in Ukumehame Gulch is the result of a single cow! (bottom left) This pregnant nanny goat (*Capra hircus*) speaks for herself.

Goat erosion, Kahakuloa Heads, West Maui. Soils are dry, lacking in topsoil, unproductive, and erodable after rains.

Axis deer (*Axis axis*)—originally from the upper Ganges region of India—were first brought to Hawai'i as a present to King Kamehameha V, released on Moloka'i in 1867. Maui deer arrived in 1959, with no one understanding what a great impact they would eventually have on native habitats.

# Native Birds

Hawai'i is famous for its spectacular diversification of one particular bird group, the Hawaiian honeycreepers, now considered to be aberrant finches (Family *Fringillidae*, subfamily *Drepanidinae*, 14 species). Counting recently extirpated species, Hawai'i housed 127 native species and subspecies of birds, of which 82 percent were endemic (found nowhere else on earth). Honeycreepers present on West Maui are illustrated on this page. Other common forest birds are the introduced Northern Cardinal and Japanese White-eye.

Robert Western

**'Apapane (*Himatione sanguinea*) is Hawai'i's commonest honeycreeper. Five inches long, its main characteristics are a red body, white undertail coverts, and black flight feathers. Watch for it sucking nectar from the red pompon blossoms of 'ōhi'a lehua or other flowering trees.**

Eric Nishibayashi

Eric Nishibayashi

**(left) Less common is the 'I'iwi (*Vestiaria coccinea*), a dazzling scarlet honeycreeper with black wings and a curved yellowish beak. (right) Also common, the insectivorous common 'amakihi differ from the similar Japanese White-eye (*Zosterops japonicus*) by the absence of a white eye-ring. Its body plumage is yellowish-green with a black band between the bill and eye.**

Hawai'i's endangered upland goose, Nēnē (*Nesochen sandvicensis*) is normally associated with Haleakalā (East Maui); however, breeding programs have increased its numbers, and it is now seen occasionally on West Maui.

(left) Owing to the presence of introduced, disease-carrying mosquitoes, native birds are only occasionally seen below 3,000 feet elevation, the approximate upper elevational limit for mosquitoes. This 'Apapane (*Himatione sanguinea*) was—quite amazingly—found on the forest floor, a victim of avian pox, the bird equivalent of smallpox. Note the large growths on its legs. (right) Hawai'i's endemic race of the Mainland United States Short-eared Owl (*Asio flammeus sandwichensis*) is primarily diurnal, periodically seen sleeping over grasslands. The Pueo was revered as an 'aumakua (guardian spirit) in old Hawai'i.

# CHAPTER 8 KĀʻANAPALI

Centuries ago the coast and hills surrounding Kāʻanapali (pron. ka-ah-nah-pah-lee) were clothed in native dryland and mesic forests—sacred ʻōhiʻa trees from which spiritual carvings were sculpted, ʻākia shrubs which yielded fish poison and tough cordage, wiliwili trees from which small surfboards were fashioned, and ʻilima, whose tiny yellow flowers were strung into royal lei. Birdlife was abundant, including several species of flightless geese and ibises. Seabirds nested in vast colonies from shore to forest, while on the beaches green turtles dug nests and monk seals lazed around with their pups.

After the early Hawaiians moved in, the area grew in cultural and historical richness, but the precious ʻāina (land) was not resilient after disturbance. Fires, in particular, resulted in a permanent loss of woodland cover and many plant species which were dependent upon shade for their survival. By the time the first explorers arrived in the late eighteenth century the land was "so parched from its southern exposure to the powerful heat of the (sun's) rays…its scorched and shriveled produce of grass and herbage (was) incapable of any kind of cultivation" (Menzies, Journal of Vancouver's Voyage 1790–94).

From the late eighteenth century, the history of West Maui is fairly well documented (also see Chapter 6). Like history anywhere, times were not always pleasant. Naturally, while this area was the focus of royal activities, a stock of myths and tales developed, some of which still survive. Hawaiians have always thrived on storytelling. In ancient times they were called moʻolelo; today one simply "talks story." Several stories center around Black Rock (see Sheraton Hotel) and the sleeping stone (see Maui Eldorado Condominium).

The names of three prominent Maui chiefs who made history here—Piʻilani, Kekaulike, and Kahekili—are well-remembered today. Piʻilani and his son Kiha (fifteenth century) left the most constructive impression, as they widened the ancient trail (alaloa) from Hāna to Kāʻanapali, portions of which can still be seen today. Two highways (unjoined) around the southern flanks of Haleakalā are still called Piʻilani Highway.

Kekaulike established a powerful kingdom on Maui which he ruled for over 50 years in the eighteenth century. During his reign Maui's people and lands became terribly impoverished, a legacy later documented by early Western explorers.

**(opposite) Dancers with kālihi at a Lei Day (May 1st) celebration.** Kāʻanapali Beach Resort

Kahekili, the last of Maui's traditional aliʻi or royalty, also inherited the warrior spirit of his forebears. During his 25-year reign (late eighteenth century) Kahekili conquered all the major islands except Hawaiʻi (Big Island), but today most of his bloody battles are forgotten, and he is remembered primarily for his daring leaps off Black Rock. His name is immortalized in Kahekili Highway, the coastal road which skirts West Maui's northern flanks.

In 1824 kiawe was introduced to Hawaiʻi from Peru. Preadapted to semidesert conditions, it spread into the dry West Maui foothills, creating vast unproductive stretches of spiny scrubland. Free-range feral goats nibbled voraciously at every green shoot, finishing off most of the original vegetation. A few native plant species struggle to survive today, assisted by their Rare and Endangered status.

In the 1840s the slopes and lowlands around Kāʻanapali were converted into sugar fields, worked by imported Asian laborers. Because sugar requires enormous amounts of water to be commercially productive (240 gallons per pound), almost all of West Maui's streams have been diverted for irrigation and no longer flow to the ocean. The area remained primarily agricultural until 1960.

Today it is difficult to visualize Kāʻanapali's former remoteness. When I first "journeyed" there from Kahului in the early '60s—an entire day's outing—the road was mostly dusty and unpaved. The upcoming Sheraton Hotel was front-page news and excited school children were taken on field trips there to witness such a colossal building!

From 1960–1990 immense changes occurred. The once isolated beaches and bays metamorphosed into a developer's (and tourist's) dream: 600 acres of landscaped hotels, condominiums, golf courses, roads, shops, and restaurants

Every effort is made to delight the visitor. Acres of lush tropical vegetation, waterfalls, pools, fountains, glorious ocean views, first-rate art, varied entertainment, attractive waitresses, scrumptious food, babysitting services, and an orchid on every pillow…all are offered with an international air of elegance. The very best aspects of Hawaiian and Pacific traditions are presented: crafts demonstrations and classes, music, dance, and an appreciation of historical events and sacred sites. For business and conference delegates, multitudinous amenities such as notary services, Japanese translation, and state-of-the-art office equipment are available. For sports enthusiasts, there are large tennis facilities, championship golf fairways, windsurfing, snorkeling, swimming, sailing, whale watching, fitness rooms, discos, catamarans, and three miles of wide, golden beaches for lazing around in the sun.

Hawaiian artist Herb Kawainui Kane is indispensable in preserving a pictorial awareness of ancient times. Every detail is culturally and geographically accurate. Here he has recreated a village scene at Keka'a, the present location of Kā'anapali resort. An auspicious omen, a rainbow, hovers over the West Maui foothills. In bygone days rainbows acted as bridges connecting the heavens and earth or spanning different islands, thus allowing unrestricted travel of humans, gods, and demigods.

(above left) Kā'anapali's shoreline from offshore. Note Black Rock at far left. (above right) Fiberglass one-man paddling canoes lie ready for launching at Hanaka'ō 'ō, Canoe Beach Park, immediately south of Kā'anapali. Park between mile markers 23 and 24. (left) Wahikuli Wayside Park— nice little roadside strip of beach, picnic tables, and lawn—is popular with local families.

Kāʻanapali's golden beaches, three miles of them, need no introduction. Although wide and scenic, with summer temperatures averaging 77°F in the morning and 82°F in the afternoon, they slope unevenly underwater, so be careful. If the shorebreak is intimidating, keep away. Suspended coral debris can cut feet, causing infections. Never turn your back on waves; even small breakers can knock adults head over heels. Use sunscreen lotions; Maui's sun is strong even in "winter." Leave earrings, watches, wallets, and other valuables in a safe place, preferably away from the beach. Public access to Kāʻanapali Beach is difficult because of limited parking. Concerned Maui residents are currently working to procure easier beach access for residents. (above right) Black Rock, an excellent snorkeling and swimming spot, and Kāʻanapali Beach.

Brett Simison

Canoe paddlers Sylvelin Kepler (left) and Pamela Dodson (right) enjoy a workout in their modern, lightweight "one-man outriggers" in preparation for upcoming competitions.

# Snorkeling

A journey into the underwater world is a special experience that can be enjoyed by nearly everyone. Clear waters and relatively gentle swimming please novice and experienced snorkelers alike at Kāʻanapali. Black Rock is best. Here are a few pointers that will set your mind at ease and help to protect this fragile environment:

1. Don't worry about sharks. Hawaiʻi's inshore waters are essentially free of dangerous sharks during the daytime. Dusk or night snorkeling is not recommended, as tiger sharks occasionally swim close to shore after dark.
2. Don't poke your fingers into, or enter, holes or caves. Hawaiʻi has several species of moray eels and lobsters that hurt people. Leave cave exploration to those with experience.
3. Don't touch sea urchins, especially the big black ones with long, skinny spines. Stings from their needles are painful.
4. Don't walk or even rest your feet on the coral reef or on rocks covered with marine life. Marine invertebrate animals (especially corals) are fragile and easily crushed.
5. Don't venture into surge channels or crevices when the sea is rough. The sea is powerful, and even small waves can bash your body against rocks, causing scrapes and cuts. Grazed skin from coral cuts is particularly painful and prone to infection.

Snorkeling gear can be rented at all resorts. Prescription masks and underwater cameras may be available.

(above left) Mamo or Hawaiian sergeant fish (*Abudefduf abdominalis*), common and stripey. (above right) Hāpuʻu or Hawaiian black grouper (*Epinephalus quernus*), is the marine equivalent of hāpuʻu tree ferns (*Cibotium spp*).

Manini or Convict tang is well known to all snorkelers in Hawaiʻi. Its name harks back to olden days when prisoners were supplied with black-striped shirts to identify their incarcerated status.

An unusual, skinny reef fish, widespread geographically, is the Chinese Trumpet fish (*Aulostoma chinensis*, or nūnū). The round-bodied, yellow reef fish in this photo include lemon butterflyfish (*Chaetodon miliaris*), raccoon butterfly fish (*Chaetodon lunula*), and fourspot butterfly fish. In past times, fish such as these were caught abundantly in circular throw nets.

Foraging in different areas of the coralheads are three common reef fish: (left to right) large blue parrotfish (*Sacrus perspicillatus*), Moorish idol (*Zanclus cornutus*), and yellowtail wrasse (*Coris gaimardi*). The last species sometimes buries itself in the bottom sand when resting.

Kā'anapali is abundantly and beautifully landscaped. (For more flowers see Chapters 3 and 6).

**Hybrid hibiscus come in a plethora of colors and patterns every year, increasing in variety. Hybrids are larger and frillier than single hibiscus flowers.**

**Glorious billowy masses of rainbow shower trees (*Cassia x nealiae*) color summer landscaping.**

**A ubiquitous landscaping ornamental is the octopus tree (*Brassaia actinophylla*), whose long floral arms mimic those of its marine namesake. Even when not blooming, this Australian curiosity is easily recognized by its umbrella-shaped, radially divided leaves. A popular house plant the world over, you may have a miniature version in your living room or office. Some local lei makers craft complex spiral lei from their round, red, knobby fruits.**

**The huge parasols of dazzling scarlet blossoms and lacy foliage sprinkled liberally around Kā'anapali are royal poincianas (*Delonix regia*).**

# Protected Marine Species

This section highlights two very special Protected Marine species: the Hawaiian green sea turtle (*Chelonia mydas*), endangered but spotted daily by delighted snorkelers on West Maui at several locations, and the Hawaiian monk seal (*Monachus schaunslandi*), a critically endangered marine mammal present in Maui's waters. Approximately 70 seals now reside in the main Hawaiian Islands and sightings are increasing.

Jack Noble / Greenpeace

**(above and below) Over the last 20 years, through collaborative research efforts, enforcement of endangered species regulations, and the purposeful release of turtles around the main islands, Hawai'i's honu or green sea turtle is finally increasing in numbers. No turtle soup on fancy menus any more in Hawai'i! Almost all of these ancient reptiles in Hawai'i's waters were born at French Frigate Shoals, a far-flung atoll 500 miles northwest of Honolulu in the Northwest Hawaiian Islands Wildlife Refuge.**

This photo was taken on Laysan Island, a rough six-day ride by small tuna boat northwest of Honolulu. I include it here because in 1994, 21 young males were released around the main islands by National Marine Fisheries personnel. Like sea turtles, most seals reside in the NW Hawaiian Islands, but Maui supports a few residents that periodically poke up their heads in surf or lumber ashore.

(left) A napping 'ilio holo i ka uaua (dog running in rough waters) and (right) monk seal tracks in the sand. An endangered species, its population totals 1,300. Compare seal and turtle tracks.

# Project Mālama Honokōwai

Project Mālama Honokōwai is in actuality a Hawaiian kupuna: a reservoir of knowledge, spiritual, mental, and physical. In Honokōwai Valley, just inland of the Sugar Cane Train station at Kāʻanapali, lies an ancient past coupled with activities related to contemporary love of the ʻāina (land). The Project's vision is to restore the valley to a state of balance, enabling it to become a place of learning and appreciation of Hawaiian culture, archaeology, and native flora. This is a special place of aloha (love, heartfelt compassion, warmth) and its companion, mālama. (Mālama means torch and mālama means to preserve, to honor, to share, to be a custodian.)

A rare, endemic hibiscus, kokiʻo ʻula varies in flower color from orange through scarlet-cerise. Remnant plants remain on West Maui.

A candlenut or kukui tree (*Aleurites moluccana*) frames restored ancient stone walls. *Ka malu halau loa o ke kukui* (a kukui grove shelters like a house).

ʻIhi (*Portulaca molokiniensis*), another rare Hawaiian plant, endemic to Molokini Islet and Kahoʻolawe, was recognized as a new species in the late 1970s by forester Bob Hobdy.

Noni (*Morinda citrifolia*), a Polynesian cure-all, belongs in the coffee family.

The unusually fragrant, stunning koki'o ke'oke'o (*Hibiscus waimeae*), another rare species, is endemic to northern Kaua'i, but now grown extensively in the state, thanks to propagation efforts.

(left) The pompon-flowered 'ōhi'a lehua (*Metrosideros polymorpha*), dominant in Hawai'i's rain forests, provided wood for religious carvings. (right) Black 'awa (*Piper methysticum*) was the highest quality soporific common to most Oceanic cultures.

A very special, rarely encountered adze sharpening stone, which helped to clear the land for the valley's 600 inhabitants centuries ago.

# Common Land Birds of West Maui

Regretfully, it is impossible to spot Hawai'i's extremely interesting—and world famous—land birds without venturing above 3,000 feet into native forests. This is due to various introduced avian diseases, notably avian malaria and pox (the bird equivalent of smallpox). Thus we must be content with an eclectic mix of Asian, American, and European immigrants. At least most are approachable and common!

(left) The Red-crested or Brazilian Cardinal (*Paroaria coronata*) is an uncommon, striking finch sporting a crimson head with jazzy crest. Look for it foraging on lawns. (right) More common is the familiar US Northern Cardinal (*Cardinalis cardinalis*), which prefers shrubbery and trees. Females are browner than males (pictured).

(left) The tiny green, white eye-ringed Japanese White-eye (*Zosterops japonicus*) almost passes for a native bird because it would be if Hawai'i was located at a more southwest latitude! A Japanese species introduced from Japan to O'ahu in 1929, adapted remarkably to Hawai'i's climate and varied habitats. Endearing itself to residents, many still call it by its original name, *mejiro*. (right) Noisy, bold, perky, and ubiquitous, the Common Mynah (*Acridotheres tristis*) pecks at fruit, nests in house gutters, congregates en masse in banyan trees, and generally unendears itself to residents. It was originally introduced from India to control insects and pests in sugarcane fields.

Another urban bird, the House or English Sparrow (*passer domesticus*), hails from Europe/Northern Asia. On O'ahu, in 1871, several pairs were released from New Zealand, where they had been previously introduced from Britain. Omnivorous, it feeds on seeds, insects, and table scraps. Check for it at outdoor restaurants.

(above) The abundant Barred or Zebra Dove (*Geopelia striata*), along with its larger kin, Spotted, Lace-necked, or Chinese Dove (*Streptopelia chinensis*) (above right), please astute listeners with their soft coos. Watch for them along less traveled roads. (right) Warbling Silverbills (*Lonchura malabarica*), with small, seed-eating, finch-like bills, travel in tight flocks of 20 or more birds. They prefer dry grassy roadsides and cane fields.

# CHAPTER 9 KAPALUA TO NĀKĀLELE

When traveling north from Kāʻanapali, the tourist bustle quickly opens out into verdant agricultural lands (primarily pineapple and coffee) sloping remarkably gently from mauka (mountainside) foothills to substantial sea cliffs. This is Kapalua: an area of refreshing breezes and a cooler atmosphere than further south, the result of trade winds wrapping around the north end of West Maui. It is an isolated haven of elegant resorts and a superb, sheltered shoreline that includes secluded golden beaches, rugged rocky promontories, a world-class surfing break, Protected Marine Parks (Honolua Bay-Mokulēʻia Marine Conservation District, 45 acres, established in 1978) and another newly protected 4.5 acre oceanfront parcel at Mokulēʻia Bay, again donated by Maui Land & Pineapple Company, and legally protected by the Maui Coastal Land Trust. The views of Molokaʻi are unparalleled.

Greater Kapalua is swathed by 23,000 acres of pineapple plantations and vegetated lands with patches of native plants. Maui Land & Pineapple Company, with a history of watershed conservation, is currently pursuing further conservation projects, including the creation of coastal and valley trails, renewable energy systems and further diversified agriculture to keep their corner of West Maui green.

Incidentally, pineapples belong in the bromeliad family, native to tropical America. Their spiny, leafy tops indicate drought resistance; however, the commercial cultivar Smooth Cayenne produces its most succulent fruits when well watered. Many tiny purple flowers rapidly coalesce during development.

Kapalua Bay Hotel

**Crescentic, golden Kapalua, or Oneloa (long sands) Beach, is protected on both ends by rocky points. It is thus safe for swimming, even in winter.**

Harrington Photo / Kapalua Bay Hotel

**Kapalua Bay Resort complex, with a mitten shaped rocky promontory separating Oneloa and Honokahua bays.**

**(opposite) Dripping with natural sugars, pineapples (*Ananas comosus*) are best picked when fully ripe; if picked green, they taste "green" and acidic, lacking full-bodied sweetness. All that is left of the multiple coalesced flowers are the little prickly "eyes."**

# Mokulēʻia, Honokōhau Marine Preserves & Nākālele Blowhole

Honolua Bay, three miles past Kapalua, is one of the prime surfing breaks in the world. Although the bay encloses a relatively small area, its waves, generated from winter swells focusing into a narrow bay, are considered perfect. When the surf is "happening," you can sit atop the cliffs and admire shapely, curling mounds of water energy as they roll gracefully toward shore. What an exquisite pale turquoise color at the apex of the wave just as it begins to break! The dazzling riders at Honolua may well be your favorite stars (pictured is Maui boy Brad Lewis). This bay was once the headquarters of Honolua Ranch, active from 1892–1914 when the first pineapples were planted.

(above) Mokulēʻia (in error Makuleʻia) Bay, locally dubbed Slaughterhouse Beach, was named for a small, cliffside slaughterhouse, now defunct. Na Ala Hele, a stairway, provides public access to the marine preserve here. Nearby beaches include D. T. Fleming Beach Park, Honokahua Bay, often windy and dangerous when seas are high.

Douglas Peebles

Honolua Bay on a calm day. It is an underwater refuge, fine for summertime snorkeling, but don't venture out in winter unless you've had experience in rough seas. Fishing, including use of spear guns, is illegal here.

Frank Rust

(left) Looking southwest, droopy ironwood trees (*Casuarina equise-tifolia*), originally from Australia, frame Mokulē'ia cliffs. During calm weather you can snorkel along these coasts. (above) Gold tree (*Tabebuia donnell-smithii*), a joy in springtime, produces great clusters of golden flowers before the leaves appear. Its bark is pale gray.

Lofty Honokōhau Falls plunge from dizzying heights (1,120 feet), epitomizing West Maui's rugged valleys not far distant from the perimeter road but impossible to reach by hiking. Although the West Maui massif is highly eroded into precipitous valleys like this, it is nonetheless a vital resource, providing precious water for lowland agriculture and residential areas only a few miles away.

From 1977–1988, the US Fish & Wildlife Service conducted comprehensive biological surveys throughout Hawaii. This baseline inventory pinpointed management priorities, today actively pursued by the West Maui Mountains Watershed Partnership and other private and public entities.

Steep, steep country: Honokōhau Valley, looking toward Kahakuloa Heads (far left). This country is for water replenishment, native wildlife. Honokōhau Valley is where the good road ends. Turn around here, since the very narrow, potholed, twisting road ahead deteriorates rapidly. Passing other "adventurers" is dangerous. Please be aware that traffic problems out here in the country are very annoying to local families who treasure their privacy.

Cameron Kepler

Rocky lava and rough waters characterize this far north sector of West Maui. Coastal topography changes here from Leeward to Windward, from relatively flat to a jumbled mass of valleys and ridges tumbling into the ocean.

(left) If you are still driving, do turn around at Nākālele Point, 18 miles north of Lahaina. The ground is dry and heavily eroded by goats, but a tenuous trail leads to a blowhole and extensive tidepool ledges. Be careful; many accidents have happened here. (right) A moist, lava-derived sinkhole and native plants are other attractions at Nākālele Point. Most coastal plants creep low because of constant trade winds.

# CHAPTER 10
# NORTH COAST & VALLEYS

To drive completely around West Maui's wet north coast you must turn around, return to Wailuku on Route 30 and start afresh on Routes 33 and 34 (340). The first interesting spot, apart from macadamia nut orchards, is the Haleki'i Pihana Heiaus State Monument off Waiehu Beach Road, Route 34. Here repose the remains of two heiau or places of worship that were converted to war temples by Maui's last ruling chief, Kahekili.

The highways promise easy travel as you pass through the former sugar plantation towns of Waiehu and Waihe'e, after which the road disintegrates rapidly, becoming a twisty, dusty, pitted, cliff-top route which resembles the old Hāna Highway. If you lived in Waihe'e a few decades ago, a village bell, now housed at the Maui Historical Society in Wailuku, would have awakened you daily at 4:30 a.m. Today, this small town houses many Filipinos, Maui's most recent immigrant group. Annual Filipino events include the Miss Maui Filipina pageant and ethnic dances in which beautiful girls, mostly tiny and slender, dress in traditional butterfly-sleeved costumes and dance to joyous folk music.

West Maui's rocky northern coastline is devoid of sandy beaches, but its indented sea cliffs (up to 450 feet high), offshore islands, and natural grandeur make it unique. Kaemi Island and Makawana Point are pictured, showing distant Kahului Harbor.

**(opposite) A clump of wild taro adds a Polynesian touch to this canyon hidden within West Maui's labyrinthine recesses. Plunging to depths up to 3,000 feet, such cliffs rarely receive direct sunlight.**

West Maui's most prominent coastal feature is Kahakuloa Head, the "tall lord," a volcanic dome as tall as a 60-story building. Once referred to as Maui's Gibraltar, Kahakuloa stands guard over a tiny village of the same name, so rural it only received electricity in the 1950s.

The tip of west Maui, showing Kahakuloa (left) and Honokōhau valleys (right) is one of the first sights that millions of people see when flying to Maui. Some say that Maui's nickname, Valley Isle, refers to the island's numerous, deeply carved valleys characteristic of West Maui's mountains. Others say that the wide valley (actually an isthmus) between Haleakalā and West Maui prompted the name. Take your choice.

Cameron Kepler

The noble profiles of two striking monoliths, Kahakuloa Head (545 feet) and Puʻu Kāhuliʻanapa (545 feet) are seen in dawn light from Mōkeʻehia, a nearby island. Nestled within their steep bluffs, a few extremely rare native plants may be found.

Mōkeʻehia Island from Hakuheʻe Point. Although only a stone's throw from the "mainland," this rocky stack supports sea-birds such as Wedge-tailed Shearwaters since it is predator-free.

An aerial view of straight-headed Kaemi Island, a special seabird breeding/roosting site.

A shore crab, *Grapsus grapsus,* vacated this shell by bursting its seams.

# Seabirds on Offshore Islands

A Wedge-tailed Shearwater chick (*Puffinus pacificus*), Hulu Island. Because of its wailing courtship calls, ancient Hawaiians named it 'Ua'u kani (moaning petrel). The people of old recognized its kinship with the 'Ua'u (*Pterodroma hawaiiensis*) which nests in Haleakalā Wilderness Area.

Cameron Kepler

(above left) Ron Lester, assisting in a West Maui seabird survey, tenderly holds a Wedge-tailed Shearwater chick. Its fuzzy, silvery down exudes a characteristic "seabird odor." (above right) Wedge-tail burrows with distant Kahakuloa Heads. (left) A pair of sleek Wedge-tailed Shearwaters. In flight, they soar low, gracefully, and in bounding arcs.

Mean-faced, weasel shaped, and rapacious, the introduced small Indian mongoose (*Herpestes auropunctatus*) gorges on every bird possible, including backyard chickens and ducks.

(right) A small, very uncommon seabird, Bulwer's Petrel or 'Ou (*Bulweria bulwerii*), spends each day at sea, returning to a small, loose colony after dark. (right bottom) Bulwer's Petrel chicks, mantled with sooty down, are raised in angular rock crevices near sea level. Throughout Hawai'i, seabird nesting is virtually restricted to offshore islands because of predatory rats and mongooses. (below) Precipitously rocky Mōke'ehia Island provides marginal nesting habitat for seabirds, but it is mongoose-free.

David Boynton

(left) Small numbers of Great Frigatebirds or ʻIwa (*Fregata minor*) cruise the cliffs and adjacent waters of West Maui's north coast. Offshore islands are their favorite roosting places; nesting occurs in the Northwest Hawaiian Islands. (right) Starkly white and elegant, White-tailed Tropicbirds or Koaʻe kea (*Phaethon lepturus*) are the only seabirds nesting on Maui with no fear of predators: they wisely choose puka (holes) in inaccessible inland cliffs.

David Boynton

(above left and above) Brown Noddies or Noio kōhā (*Anous stolidus*) commonly form small flocks, feeding inshore on small subsurface fish. The Hawaiian name means plump noddy tern. (left) Black/Hawaiian Noddies or Noio (*Anous minutus*), also foraging along rocky coastlines, can be distinguished from Brown Noddies by black (not brown) plumage, whiter crown, thinner beak, and smaller overall size. Perfect identification takes practice!

# Waihe'e Valley

Waihe'e has long been recognized as one of the four major valleys termed Na Wai 'ehā (The Four Streams). Also including Waiehu, 'Īao, and Waikapū valleys, in precontact times this multi-tributaried watershed drained about one quarter of West Maui's land mass from its topmost serpentine ridges clear to the ocean.

Looking mauka (upslope), Waihe'e Valley. This broad, multibranched stream complex contrasts sharply with other West Maui valleys, which become increasingly narrow as they progress inland. Na Wai 'ēha was formerly the largest contiguous area of wet taro cultivation in Hawai'i.

(left) ʻŌhiʻa lehua (*Metrosideros polymorpha*), Hawaiʻi's beloved forest tree, is common along the spectacular (but rigorous) Waiheʻe Ridge Trail, which climbs to Lanilili Peak (2,563 feet) from Camp Maluhia Boy Scout Camp (almost mile marker 7, Hwy 340 heading north). Northwards lies a huge chunk of West Maui Natural Area Reserve. Since earliest colonization, ʻōhiʻa has figured prominently in the legends and religion of the Hawaiian people. For centuries it was used primarily for carving temple images, enclosures, and war gods. Easy to whittle when fresh, it was carved only by skilled craftsmen who were well-versed in religious ritual and carpentry.

John Carothers

(above left and above) The endemic, yet common kanawao (*Broussaisia arguta*), Hawaiʻi's sole member of the hydrangea family, bears variably colored flowers in flowerheads reminiscent of cultivated hydrangeas. The male flowers at right boast abundant, conspicuous stamens. (left) ʻŌhā wai (*Clermontia kakeana*). Waiheʻe Ridge Trail is a prime area to observe this green-and-purple flowered beauty, one of Hawaiʻi's famous lobelias. It begins blooming in May continuing through the summer.

One of Hawai'i's most stunning traditional banana varieties, Iholena Kāpua, photo-graphed in the wild (left) and in cultivation (right). This precious heirloom, used medicinally as well as for food, was carried northwards from Tahiti 600–800 years ago. Note its long, graceful, dark red fruit stalk and and short-tapered fruit tips.

John Carothers

Water erosion and volcanicity. One needs little imagination to relive these tremendous forces of nature here, where cascade-worn buttresses fall steeply into Waihe'e Valley. Haleakalā's 10,000-foot volcanic mound forms an impressive backdrop. Hikers can enjoy views such as this from the Waihe'e Ridge Trail, which is two miles long, uphill all the way.

Lovely Waihe'e Valley Trail (Swinging Bridges) (Call Wailuku Agribusiness 808-244-9570 for permission), is un-suitable for those who balk at rickety bridges. Marvel at the hand-hewing brawn of Chinese workers who hacked out irrigation ditches to divert stream water to sugarcane fields in the 1800s.

# Waiheʻe Preserve

Maui's newest preserve, Waiheʻe Coastal Dunes and Wetlands Preserve (Waiheʻe Preserve) is a credit to all who fought hard for its acquisition. Its spectacular location and varied habitats embrace 277 acres of coastal, spring-fed wetlands, dune ecosystems, riparian (stream) habitats, and 1.3 miles of shoreline. In addition to common plants and animals, at least seven endangered life forms have so far been spotted: Green turtle, Hawaiian Coot and Stilt, two coastal plants, and two insects.

An ancient fishing village, heiau (temple site) and sizable burial sites are in the process of recovery and restoration. Within the preserve's clear blue offshore waters, marine life is rich because of 1) Waiheʻe Reef, one of the largest on Maui, 2) limited fishermen, and 3) relatively sparse urban development upslope.

The Maui Coastal Land Trust's mission of preserving and protecting coastal lands of Maui Nui for the benefit of the natural environment and also for current and future generations, meshes well here—and elsewhere on Maui—with similar goals of The Nature Conservancy, West Maui Mountains Watershed Partnership, and other state and community-based nonprofit organizations. The preserve is best visited by appointment (call 808-244-5263), reached on Hwy 340 north from Wailuku.

Ron Chapple / Blue Hawaiian Helicopters

**An outlined perspective of Waiheʻe Preserve illustrates its wide range of habitats, terrestrial and marine.**

(above) The low-lying, spring-fed wetlands vary their water levels according to rainfall and spring flow. (above right) In 2003, a host of community volunteers cleared this lovely beach shore of tons of flotsam and jetsam. Waiheʻe Preserve includes 1.3 miles of sandy and cobbled beaches, ideal feeding grounds for migratory shorebirds and nesting sites for endangered green turtles (right).

Endangered Hawaiian Stilts and Coots frequently forage in the preserve's swampy pond, presided over by 10,000-foot Haleakalā.

The endangered Aeʻo or Black-necked Hawaiian Stilt (*Himantopus mexicanus knudseni*), totaling only 1,800 birds, has few feeding and breeding sites left in the entire state of Hawaiʻi. On Maui, they also occur at Keālia and Kanahā ponds in Māʻalaea and Kahului, respectively. Note those brilliant slender, cerise legs!

# Native Coastal Plants

West Maui's north shore is one of the few areas on Maui where native coastal plants can still be found. Don't expect pristine habitats: Given the area's history of extensive land clearance for sugar, cattle, and coffee, they might be either weedy or goat eroded, but a curious plant watcher will be rewarded, especially near Nākālele Blowhole and the Waihe'e Preserve.

**(above) Famous in folklore, beach naupaka or naupaka kahakai (*Scaevola sericea*) is generally a bush, but here on windswept, goat-eroded slopes it hugs the ground. Succulent, salt-tolerant leaves and styrofoam-like white berries (huahekili or hailstones) equip it for coastal survival.**

**(above left) Creeping or flat 'ilima, 'ilima papa (*Sida fallax*) also crawls stealthily along dry ground, periodically poking up tiny yellow, hibiscus-like flowers which were formerly used by Hawaiians for lei making. (above right) Nehe (*Lipochaeta integrifolia*), a tiny-leaved member of the daily family, prefers sandy substrates, rooting from nodes as it creeps along. (left) The clustered, white, rose-like flowers and rosehip-like fruits of 'ūlei (*Osteomeles anthyllidifolia*) reveal its botanical affinities.**

(left) A hardy, viney shrub, 'ūlei cascades over road banks and moist coastal cliffs on West Maui's north shore. Even today, lei artisans use its attractive divided leaf tips for haku-style lei. (right) Dotted with little pale blue bells, pa'u o Hi'iaka is a delicately flowered morning glory vine. Its name, The Skirt of Hi'iaka, echoes a folktale wherein this vine protected a special baby from the scorching sun by rapidly blanketing it.

(left) Dwarf naupaka or false jade plant (*Scaevola coriacea*), Endangered, sports a curious half-flower like its relative, beach naupaka (see page 154). Very rare, here it embellishes a Wedge-tailed Shearwater burrow on Mōke'ehia Island (right).

(left) A wind-pruned, pointy-leaved 'ākia bush (*Wikstroemia uva-ursi*) lies completely prostrate. (right) 'Akoko (*Chamaesyce degeneri*), round-leaved with yellow, poinsettia-like flowers, acts likewise. This is really windy country!

# Introduced Roadside Plants of West Maui

    Many of the following plants grow beside roads throughout West Maui, but because there is more variety on the north shore, I have placed the section here. Basically, roadsides are dominated by introduced plants— some pretty, some of little visual worth. However, plants whisper to us of their Maui origins, of their struggles to survive, of culture and land use. For example, entrepreneurs grew commercial coffee here long ago. By the mid-1800s it was widely cultivated in the region's moist valleys where remnant groves still exist. Sisals, the large spiny "century plants" clinging to barren cliffs and hillsides, are not runaway garden ornaments; they remind us of former heydays of rope-making, when whaling ships needed hawsers and rigging lines and the developing cattle industry needed fodder.

Frank Rust

**A sheltered roadside seep nourishes a bank of delicate maidenhair ferns (*Adiantum raddianum*), while touch-me-nots (*Impatiens suttoni*) add a splash of pink. Although this maidenhair, the commonest species in Hawai'i, looks native, regretfully it is not. It aggressively displaced Hawai'i's native 'iwa'iwa (*Adiantum capillus-veneris*), formerly widespread but now extremely rare.**

(left) This nasty spined century plant is actually the renowned sisal (*Agave sisal*), once commercially raised on West Maui for ship's hawsers, binder twine for grain, and even for hula skirts. Its mineral-rich leaf waste found uses as fertilizer and cattle feed. (right) From Peru, kiawe (*Prosopis pallida*), rich in nitrogen, is still used as cattle fodder and for delicious local honey. Watch for spines, which can be bothersome if you are barefooted.

(left and right) Like kiawe, koa haole (*Leucaena leucocephala*) has similar uses and grows in similar wasteland or dry habitats.

(left) Originally from Southeast Asia, the canoe plant kukui or candlenut tree (*Aleurites moluccana*) shades many inland valleys with its twisted trunks and maple-like leaves. (above) Pretty but pesky, the colorful, prickly lantana or lākana (*Lantana camara*), introduced from the West Indies in 1858, is an extremely serious weed in forests and pastures.

(above left) The striking kāhili flower (*Grevillea banksii*) from Australia, is sparsely naturalized north of Waiheʻe. It is related to silk oak, banksias, and proteas. (above right) Several times per year, the deliciously sweet-acid, strawberry guavas (*Psidium cattleianum*) bear fruits; they may be red or yellow. (left) Chinese violet or asystasia (*Asystasia gangetica*), with violet, funnel shaped flowers, forms dense low thickets.

(left) Strawberry guava thicket. (right) Paperbark (*Melaleuca quinquenervia*), an Australian native but introduced from Florida in 1920 and planted extensively by foresters throughout Hawai'i, is familiar to Maui hikers. It is easily recognized by its cream, eucalyptus-like, floral pompons and tissue-soft, fine, shedding bark.

(above left and right) Common everywhere except in very dry areas, Christmas berry or wilelaiki (*Schinus terebinthifolius*), native to Brazil, forms dense thickets which fruit in winter. Its berries are inedible. (left) Kolomona (*Senna surattensis*), originally from Australia, escaped from cultivated in 1871. Its pea-like, yellow-gold flowers brighten roadsides and gulches along Hwy 340. Kolomona means Solomon, a name which reflects biblical influence.

# ENVIRONMENTAL ALERT

Flowering Miconia or purple plague (*Miconia calvescens*), beginning to invade West Maui. Photo is from interior Tahiti.

Maui, situated at 21°N latitude in the oceanic subtropics, is an ideal adopted home for introduced tropical plants. Most thrive in gardens and landscaping, presenting few problems. However, some escape into natural or seminatural ecosystems and literally "run wild." The 1970s and 1980s experienced a proliferation of now-familiar pests on Maui such as strawberry guava (*Psidium cattleianum*); inkberry (*Ardisia elliptica*); yellow, white, and kāhili gingers (*Hedychium spp*); Java plum (*Syzgium cuminii*); and African tulip tree (*Spathodea campanulata*).

The 1990s ushered in more menacing species, two so virulent they are capable of completely and rapidly wiping out Maui's lowland and upland forests. The most lethal offender is miconia, Miconia calvescens, called purple plague or green cancer in Tahiti, where it has aggressively invaded forests from sea level to 4,260 feet in less than 25 years.

The other is cane tibouchina (*Tibouchina herbacea*).

Over 60 percent of the main island of Tahiti is now dominated by purple plague's thick, dark groves, which grow to 60 feet tall. Today, one-quarter of Tahiti's native plant species are nearly extinct. This invasive plant has now spread to other islands in French Polynesia, some hundreds of miles distant.

Despite enormous expenses of time and money, Maui is poised for a similar scenario. Purple plague competes with feral pigs as the most serious threat to conservation in Hawai'i. Its potential impact is far greater than all other noxious plants combined. Purple plague's continued encroachment into Maui's forests will render all past, present, and future conservation efforts futile, since it crowds out all established forms of life. Not even common birds, insects, and plants can survive its onslaught.

Purple plague's horticultural name is velvet leaf. In its native tropical America, where it colonizes light gaps, its populations are balanced by natural controls (insects, disease), absent in Hawai'i where, under favorable conditions, a three-foot square experimental plot produced 18,000 seedlings in six months! Admittedly attractive, it is esteemed for its large purple below. Note the three bold leaf veins, a characteristic of its family, *Melastomataceae*.

Lake Vaihiria, interior Tahiti. Most greenery visible is miconia.

Watch for inkberry (*Ardisia elliptica*) flowers in West Maui; they spread phenomenally on East Maui during the last 20 years. Fresh foliage is bronze-pinkish. Its star-shaped flowers are pink and its berries, red, or purple-black like tight clusters of blueberries.

Miconia has a bright purple leaf underside.

Randy Bartlett

(left) Cane tibouchina (*Tibouchina herbacea*). It is extremely important that all these noxious weeds not be further transported to and from East Maui. (right) Inkberry fruit (*Ardisia elliptica*), spread by hikers and birds.

# INDEX

# ABOUT THE AUTHOR

Howard Brownscombe

**Angela Kay Kepler admires Hawaiian varieties of kō (sugarcane) in ʻ Īao Valley State Park, West Maui, 2003.**

Dr. Angela Kay Kepler, a naturalized New Zealander, is an "old-fashioned naturalist" holding degrees from the University of Canterbury (New Zealand), University of Hawaiʻi (Honolulu), and Cornell University (New York). She also spent one year as a postdoctoral student at Oxford University, England. Angela first came to Hawaiʻi in 1963 as an East-West Center foreign student, has been a Maui kamaʻāina for 18 years, and lives in Haikū. Her multifaceted career involves field biology, writing and illustrating natural history books for the "intelligent public," and environmental consulting. An energetic, award-winning writer and photographer, backpacker, birdwatcher, ecologist, adventurer, and teacher, she has visited wilderness areas in nearly 90 countries.

Angela was involved for ten years in the US Fish & Wildlife Service Forest Bird Surveys throughout Hawaiʻi, during which she surveyed wildlife all over Maui. Her broad-based ecological research in Hawaiʻi, the Pacific Islands, and the Caribbean always focused on the preservation of prime natural areas: Continuing projects are advising the Government of Kiribati, Bishop Museum (Living Archipelagos Program), UNESCO (Central Pacific Islands World Heritage Site), and other Pacific agencies. Together with her husband, Frank Rust, she is also part of the Maui Native Banana Working Group's efforts to protect Hawaiʻi's last remaining traditional bananas.

Over the last 40 years, Angela has authored or coauthored 18 books, numerous scientific publications, and technical reports, and contributed articles and photos to Island publications. Her other books relating to Hawaiʻi include: *Maui's Hana Highway*; *Proteas in Hawaiʻi*; *Haleakalā: A Guide to the Mountain*; *Trees of Hawaiʻi*; *Exotic Tropicals of Hawaiʻi: Heliconias, Gingers, Anthuriums, and Decorative Foliage*; *Maui's Floral Splendor*; *Hawaiʻi's Floral Splendor*; *Hawaiian Heritage Plants*; *Sunny South Maui*; *Wonderful West Maui*; and *Majestic Molokaʻi*.